Seeking the Soul
Through Meditations on Draconic Astrology

By

Patricia Godden

Grosvenor House
Publishing Limited

All rights reserved
Copyright © Patricia Godden, 2023

The right of Patricia Godden to be identified as the author of this work has been asserted in accordance with Section 78 of the Copyright, Designs and Patents Act 1988

The book cover is copyright to Patricia Godden
Cover image copyright to GoodIdeas

This book is published by
Grosvenor House Publishing Ltd
Link House
140 The Broadway, Tolworth, Surrey, KT6 7HT.
www.grosvenorhousepublishing.co.uk

This book is sold subject to the conditions that it shall not, by way of trade or otherwise, be lent, resold, hired out or otherwise circulated without the author's or publisher's prior consent in any form of binding or cover other than that in which it is published and without a similar condition including this condition being imposed on the subsequent purchaser.

A CIP record for this book
is available from the British Library

ISBN 978-1-80381-364-6

With thanks to Astrolabe Inc (alabe.com) for the use of Solar Fire software in the creation of diagrams in this work.

This is a non-fiction book. The author and the publisher make no guarantees as to the accuracy of the information contained in this book. This book contains the author's views, thoughts and opinions about the soul, spirit, spirituality and draconic astrology together with descriptions of her personal experiences during meditations. The intent of the author is only to offer information of a general nature to help readers in their quest for information on the soul and spirituality. The information contained in this book may not be suitable for your situation. Readers are advised to seek independent professional advice for medical, legal, financial or other specialist questions. Neither the publisher nor the author can be held responsible for any loss, claim or damage arising out of use or misuse of information or suggestions made in this book.

Table of Contents

	Page
Introduction	ix

Chapter 1
From Tropical Horoscope to Draconic Horoscope	1
The tropical horoscope	1
The nodes of the Moon in the tropical horoscope	1
Interpreting the nodes of the Moon in the tropical horoscope	3
The draconic horoscope	4
Calculation of the draconic horoscope by hand	5
Erecting a draconic horoscope by computer	13
Dual wheels	14
Bi-wheels	14
General considerations	15
Similarities and differences between tropical and draconic charts	16

Chapter 2
Going into Meditation	17
The cave	19

Chapter 3
Meditations on the Draconic Meanings of the Planets	24
Draconic Sun	24
Draconic Moon	28

Draconic Mercury	32
Draconic Venus	36
Draconic Mars	40
Draconic Jupiter	44
Draconic Saturn	47
Draconic Uranus	52
Draconic Neptune	56
Draconic Pluto	59

Chapter 4
Meditations on the Draconic Meanings of the Signs
of the Zodiac 63

Draconic Aries	63
Draconic Taurus	65
Draconic Gemini	68
Draconic Cancer	72
Draconic Leo	75
Draconic Virgo	78
Draconic Libra	80
Draconic Scorpio	84
Draconic Sagittarius	88
Draconic Capricorn	91
Draconic Aquarius	96
Draconic Pisces	99

Chapter 5
Review	103
Some further thoughts	106

List of Figures

	Page
Figure 1. The tropical horoscope showing the positions of the Sun and Moon as well as the north node of the Moon at 15° 00′ Taurus and the south node of the Moon at 15° 00′ Scorpio.	7
Figure 2. The tropical horoscope shown in Figure 1 is in the centre and surrounded by the draconic zodiac.	9
Figure 3. The tropical horoscope showing the positions of the Sun and Moon as well as the north node of the Moon at 20° 00′ Gemini and the south node of the Moon at 20° 00′ Sagittarius.	11
Figure 4. The tropical horoscope shown in Figure 3 is in the centre and surrounded by the draconic zodiac.	12
Figure 5. The cave	21
Figure 6. Draconic Sun	27
Figure 7. Draconic Moon	30
Figure 8. Draconic Mercury	34
Figure 9. Draconic Venus	38
Figure 10. Draconic Mars	42
Figure 11. Draconic Jupiter	46
Figure 12. Draconic Saturn	50

Figure 13. Draconic Uranus	55
Figure 14. Draconic Neptune	58
Figure 15. Draconic Pluto	61
Figure 16. Draconic Aries	64
Figure 17. Draconic Taurus	67
Figure 18. Draconic Gemini	71
Figure 19. Draconic Cancer	74
Figure 20. Draconic Leo	77
Figure 21. Draconic Virgo	79
Figure 22. Draconic Libra	82
Figure 23. Draconic Scorpio	86
Figure 24. Draconic Sagittarius	90
Figure 25. Draconic Capricorn	94
Figure 26. Draconic Aquarius	98
Figure 27. Draconic Pisces	101
Figure 28. Life	108

Acknowledgements

I thank the great Beings of the planets, the White Brethren, Brothers, angels and guides for making this work possible.

Deep gratitude goes to my parents and family for their love and encouragement. I greatly appreciate the support and patience of my friends during the preparation of this book: thank you.

Introduction

This book is about seeking the soul through the means of meditation. There is nothing new in this. Meditation is a way of understanding deeper facets of the human being that has been used for millennia. In this book, the meditations have focused on draconic astrology, a particular branch of astrology which is thought to show the soul's impulses. However, before we go into detail about either meditation or astrology it is first necessary to be clear about what is meant by the word 'soul' and its relationship with 'spirit'.

SPIRIT

The dictionary defines spirit as 'the force or principle of life that animates the body or living things' (*Collins English Dictionary, Millennium Edition*). For me, the word 'spirit' has a more extensive meaning. Spirit is infinite and eternal. It is the spark of life, the immeasurable factor that is in everything including all life forms such as plants, animals and every person. I believe that spirit is also in apparently inanimate things such as the oceans, air, rocks and minerals, the Earth and the planets. It is in everything that has ever been created. The human spirit is part of spirit.

Human beings in physical bodies are the physical manifestation of the human spirit. However, in order to go from the incomprehensible dimensions of the spirit to a physical human being there needs to be some intermediary, some means of stepping down this energy to the level that a physical human being can cope with. This is done through the soul.

SOUL
The dictionary defines soul as 'the spirit or immaterial part of man, the seat of human personality, intellect, will and emotions, regarded as an entity that survives the body after death' (*Collins English Dictionary, Millennium Edition*). As with the word 'spirit', for me, the word 'soul' has a much wider meaning. The soul is that part of the human spirit that comes into incarnation in a human physical body in order to gather certain experiences of life on Earth. Through the experiences of many, many incarnations, the soul gradually learns to express spiritual qualities, which include unconditional love and infinite wisdom. When honed to perfection, these qualities can then be used in the loving and wise use of power; the use of power that is for the good of all life.

While the soul is part of spirit and spirit infuses the soul, spirit and soul are different facets of our total being.

SPIRITUAL
In the dictionary, the word 'spiritual' is defined as 'relating to the spirit or soul and not to physical nature or matter; intangible' (*Collins English Dictionary, Millennium Edition*). While the dictionary includes the concept of both spirit and soul in the term 'spiritual', in this book I use the word 'spiritual' when referring to spirit.

ASTROLOGY
Two of the many branches of astrology are called tropical astrology and draconic astrology. These are based on the

zodiacs that are used to create a horoscope. Tropical astrology uses the tropical zodiac and draconic astrology uses the draconic zodiac. Both zodiacs contain the same twelve signs from Aries to Pisces but they differ in the location of 0° Aries.

Tropical zodiac
In the tropical zodiac, 0° Aries is the point where the Sun is located at the spring equinox. It is usually on 20th or 21st March and coincides with the upsurge of energy at the beginning of the growth season in the northern hemisphere.

Tropical astrology examines the nature of a person, their personality and the opportunities and challenges they may experience. This contributes to a greater understanding of their life. Tropical astrology, when looked at esoterically, includes a spiritual interpretation.

The north node of the Moon is the point in space where the orbit of the Moon around the Earth crosses the ecliptic, which is the orbit of the Earth around the Sun. The north node of the Moon can be anywhere in the tropical zodiac depending on the time when a person was born.

Draconic zodiac
In the draconic zodiac, the north node of the Moon is set to 0° Aries. All planets are in the same relative positions to each other as in the tropical zodiac but translocated by the number of degrees between the tropical north node of the Moon and tropical 0° Aries. This is described in more detail in the first chapter. With the north node of the Moon being at

0° Aries, the draconic zodiac represents a new beginning for the soul's journey.

While I was training as an astrologer, I was told that draconic astrology relates to the soul's impulses, to deeply held values inherent in the soul, as well as spiritual promptings. The relationship between the tropical and draconic zodiacs was described as follows: tropical astrology materialises the spiritual while draconic astrology spiritualises the material. These terms raised many questions for me. I wanted to know if draconic astrology relates to the soul, spirit or the relationship between soul and spirit.

In order to answer these questions, I meditated on the planets and signs of the zodiac at the draconic level. I started to use the information from these meditations when looking at horoscopes. I explained to each client that the interpretations of the draconic part of their reading was based on information from my meditations and this information had not been verified by other astrologers. Many clients have found that the draconic part of their reading resonated with them and helped them look at deeper levels of their life.

Over several years, I began to feel that draconic astrology may manifest in a range of ways depending on the person whose horoscope is being examined. In some cases, it feels that draconic astrology is closer to the material level of life. The people for whom this applies live at the physical level of consciousness and are less interested in soul impulses or the finer vibrations and levels of life. In other cases, the soul impulses feel closer to spirit. These people are more aware of spiritual values and strive to incorporate them into their daily lives.

The different levels cannot be judged as elementary or advanced. None is better or worse than any other level. I believe that, in every case, it is the right level for that soul at its current stage of evolution; in other words, in this incarnation. Each incarnation is just one of the many, many incarnations necessary for the soul to learn and absorb all there is to learn from life on Earth.

Here are several different thoughts on why, depending on the person, a draconic horoscope could feel closer to the physical level of life or a more spiritual level.

- It may relate to the stage of evolution of the soul concerned.
- It may relate to the level of physical life that the soul needs to experience in the present incarnation to help it understand spiritual values.
- It is also possible that an advanced soul may choose to incarnate into a life lived very much at the physical level either to give a specific service on Earth or to gain a particular experience that it needs for its soul development.

There could be many other reasons too.

At my current stage of evolution, I feel I only have glimpses of what soul and spirit really are. I acknowledge that they go beyond my human comprehension. However, I do feel that in all cases the soul and spiritual levels of our being cannot be separated. More inner work is needed to fully understand the nature of the soul, the spirit and how they relate to each other and the whole of life. The meditations on the draconic level of the planets and signs of the zodiac are a very small step towards understanding this vast subject. I have no doubt that as humanity evolves the answer to this mystery will become apparent.

The most recent publication on draconic astrology at the time of writing (August 2022) is a very comprehensive book by Victor Olliver: *Chasing the Dragons: An Introduction to Draconic Astrology*. Victor looks at the draconic and tropical horoscopes of many people. Within his book, he includes, with my blessing, key phrases and summary comments from my meditations on draconic astrology, which were originally published in *The Astrological Journal* in 2017.

The book now in your hands gives a full account of my experiences during meditations on the draconic level of the planets and signs of the zodiac. It also includes thoughts from times of contemplation after the meditations that contributed to my understanding at an inner level. These experiences are described in words and illustrated with pictures I painted to capture the essence of the meditations.

At the current stage of human evolution, I feel that the first chart to examine is the tropical horoscope as it relates to the physical life lived in the material three-dimensional world. Only when there is a good understanding of the tropical chart and outer life is it possible to consider the inner life and the soul's impulses by examining the draconic horoscope. When the draconic horoscope is placed around the tropical horoscope in a bi-wheel, it is possible to get some insight into how the soul is guiding the outer life. Aspects between planets or angles in the draconic and tropical horoscopes give more information on how the soul's impulses are manifesting in the outer life.

The descriptions of the draconic level of the planets and signs given in this book can be used to interpret the draconic horoscopes of individuals, countries, international organisations and events. Draconic astrology can be used with transits, progressions and other forms of directions.

Before considering the meditations, astrologers who are not familiar with draconic astrology may wish to learn how to erect a draconic horoscope. This is covered in the first chapter. However, if your main interest is in meditation and seeking the soul, you can skip Chapter 1 and go directly to Chapter 2, Going into Meditation, and then on to the meditations themselves in Chapters 3 and 4.

Chapter 1

From Tropical Horoscope to Draconic Horoscope

Many readers will be familiar with the tropical zodiac so only the briefest description of its role is given here. The tropical nodes of the Moon are described together with how they indicate the direction of the soul's journey. There then follows a section on how to calculate the draconic horoscope and construct a bi-wheel of the tropical and draconic horoscopes. Descriptions of the meditations and the planets and signs of the zodiac at the draconic level are in the following chapters.

The tropical horoscope
In the tropical zodiac, 00° 00′ Aries signifies the outward movement into incarnation on the wheel of life. It is sometimes thought of as representing the first step away from a higher state of unity in order to learn about dualism, self and non-self, through experiences of physical life. The positions of the planets in the tropical zodiac indicate how that dualism plays out and the opportunities the soul has to learn from life in a human body.

The nodes of the Moon in the tropical horoscope
The Moon orbits the Earth anticlockwise on a plane that is inclined by 5° 09′ to the ecliptic, which is the plane of the orbit of the Earth around the Sun. The two places where the

orbit of the Moon crosses the ecliptic are called the south node of the Moon and the north node of the Moon. The nodes of the Moon can be at any opposing positions in the tropical horoscope, depending on the time of birth.

The south node of the Moon is where the Moon is moving in a southerly direction as it crosses the ecliptic. This point is sometimes called the descending node, the dragon's tail, *Cauda draconis,* or, in Vedic astrology, Rahu. The north node of the Moon is where the Moon crosses the ecliptic on the northward part of its journey around the Earth. The north node is sometimes called the ascending node, the dragon's head, *Caput draconis,* or, in Vedic astrology, Ketu.

As the Sun represents spirit, the Moon signifies the soul and the Earth relates to physical matter, the nodes of the Moon link spirit, soul and matter.

The motion of the nodes includes both retrograde and direct phases. The retrograde phase generally lasts between 4 and 39 days and the nodes move 0° 03′ – 4° 20′ retrograde during this time. After a short period of a day or so when the nodes appear to be stationary, they move 0° 01′ – 0° 05′ in direct motion over 1 – 7 days. From this it can be seen that the overall movement of the nodes of the Moon is retrograde with shorter periods of direct motion and even shorter times when they seem to be stationary as they appear to change direction.

The direction, retrograde or direct, or the lack of movement of the nodes of the Moon may be linked with the soul's impulses and purpose in life. For most people, the nodes of the Moon are retrograde. In my experience, many of these people go with the flow of life. Fewer people have the nodes travelling direct. These people may go against the norm in some way. The nodes of the Moon are stationary in the minority of people. I have found that these people can have a strong sense of purpose.

It takes 18.6129 years or 18 years, 7 months and 9 days for the nodes of the Moon to move through all 12 signs of the zodiac. They spend approximately 18 months in each sign.

Interpreting the nodes of the Moon in the tropical horoscope

The nodes of the Moon relate to the soul's experience. The soul incarnates many times before it has mastered the complete experience of life on Earth. During any one incarnation, it has the wisdom accumulated in previous incarnations. The particular part of this wisdom that is relevant to the current life is indicated by the sign and house position of the south node of the Moon in the tropical zodiac. The south node does not represent the whole of the soul's experiences.

The south node of the Moon can be thought of as part of the soul memory. Its position shows what the soul is comfortable doing because it already has some experience in this field. The qualities of this experience often manifest early in life. Even as an adult, the person may retreat to these experiences when tired or during periods of stress, possibly because they are familiar. The experience reflected in the south node of the Moon may be developed further during the current life.

When there is a focus on one primary facet of life, such as the experiences represented by the south node of the Moon, it can lead to an imbalance in the range of experiences. The soul may have created karma in these areas and subsequently wish to address it. In order to bring equilibrium and adjust any imbalance, the soul strives for complementary experiences. The nature of these new experiences and the area of life in which they may manifest are indicated by the sign of the zodiac and house position of the north node of the Moon.

The nodes of the Moon are linked with complementary experiences. Over the course of time, the soul learns more about the broad spectrum of all possible experiences and how to bring equilibrium, balance and harmony into life lived in a physical body on planet Earth. The soul learns to integrate what appear to be different perspectives on life. Wisdom and experience learned in the past, in previous incarnations, are incorporated into what the soul is striving to learn about in the present life. This enriches the soul's overall wisdom.

The draconic horoscope
The draconic zodiac has the same twelve signs of the zodiac as the tropical zodiac. In the draconic horoscope, the north node of the Moon is always at 00° 00′ Aries and the south node of the Moon at 00° 00′ Libra. This may be thought of as the drive of the soul to engage with new experiences in the light of previous experiences. The soul balances previous experiences and broadens their scope by integrating them into what it is currently striving to learn.

I believe that the draconic horoscope provides more information about the deeper impulses of the soul as well as those parts of the totality of all possible experiences within spirit that the soul has chosen to learn about in this lifetime.

With the ever-increasing experience of successive lives, somehow the draconic chart might be able to indicate the level of soul development: how 'old' the soul is and how close it is to mastering earthly life. This is way beyond what I am capable of and I would not dream of attempting to say how old any soul is. The ability to extend the interpretation of a draconic chart in this way may depend on the astrologer being a highly evolved soul. Those who founded draconic astrology may have been advanced souls or people who were inspired by very wise beings.

Calculation of the draconic horoscope by hand

It only involves some simple arithmetic to calculate the number of degrees that separate each planet in the tropical horoscope from 0° Aries. It is important to add up the number of degrees going through the signs of the zodiac in their order of Aries, Taurus, Gemini, Cancer, and so on, rather than counting backwards from Aries via Pisces and Aquarius. A planet would be 359° away from Aries if it were at 29° Pisces.

The next step is to calculate the number of degrees between 0° Aries and the position of the north node of the Moon in the tropical horoscope.

The number of degrees that separate the north node of the Moon from 0° Aries is subtracted from the number of degrees that separate each of the planets in the tropical horoscope from 0° Aries. The resulting figure is the number of degrees that lie between each planet and 0° Aries in the draconic horoscope.

This is then converted into the number of whole signs and degrees of the sign that each planet occupies in the draconic horoscope.

Thus to produce the draconic horoscope, the zodiac of the tropical horoscope is effectively turned by the number of degrees that divide the tropical north node from 0° Aries.

Example 1
It is possible to build this up in simple steps. This first example is a simple theoretical example shown in Figure 1. This shows the signs of the tropical zodiac and only the Sun and Moon. The ascendant is at 0° Aries. The nodes of the Moon can be placed over this. In this example, the north node is at 15° Taurus and the south node is at 15° Scorpio. The words 'north' and 'south' have been written on the figure because the symbol of the south node looks like that of the north node but upside down.

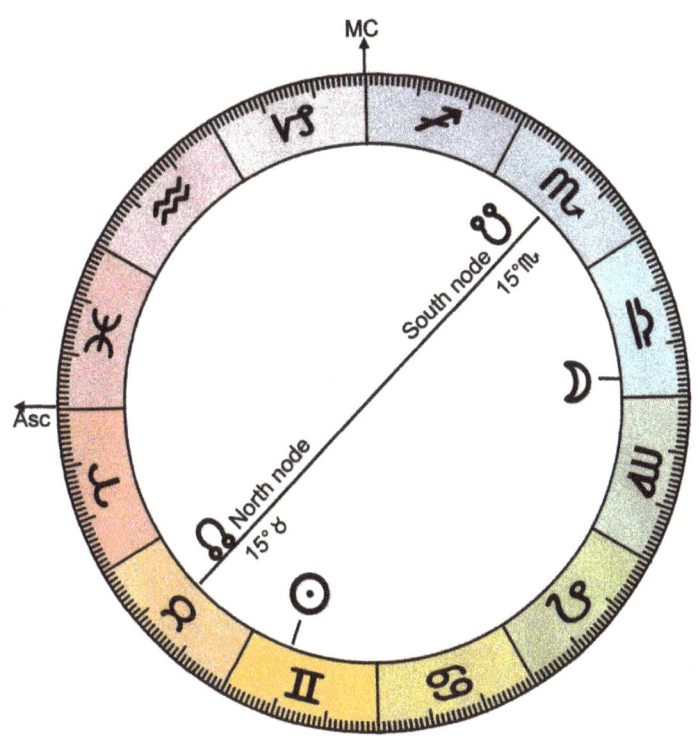

Figure 1. The tropical horoscope showing the positions of the Sun and Moon as well as the north node of the Moon at 15° 00′ Taurus and the south node of the Moon at 15° 00′ Scorpio.

Using the method of calculation described above:

	Sun	Moon
Position of planet in tropical zodiac	10° Gemini	3° Libra
Number of degrees of planet from 0° Aries in tropical zodiac	70°	183°
North node of the Moon at 15° Taurus in tropical zodiac is 45° from 0° Aries		
Position of planet minus position of north node of the Moon in the tropical zodiac = position of planet in draconic zodiac	70 - 45 25° from 0° Aries	183 - 45 138° from 0° Aries
Position of planet in draconic zodiac	25° Aries	18° Leo

The same calculation is made for the angles. The tropical ascendant is at 0° Aries. The draconic ascendant will be at 0° Aries - 45°, which is 15° Aquarius in the draconic horoscope.

    The approach to life is different in the physical and soul levels of life as indicated by the signs on the tropical and draconic ascendants. At the physical level, as indicated by the tropical ascendant in Aries, the person could be self-centred and courageous, enterprising and able to initiate action. However, the soul's impulses, as indicated by the ascendant being in Aquarius in the draconic chart, are more objective, detached and there may be humanitarian ideals. This may subtly modify how the tropical horoscope manifests.

In Figure 2, the circle of the draconic zodiac has been placed round the tropical zodiac so that 0° of draconic Aries is over the north node of the tropical zodiac. This can be done by hand if there is no access to a computer with astrology software.

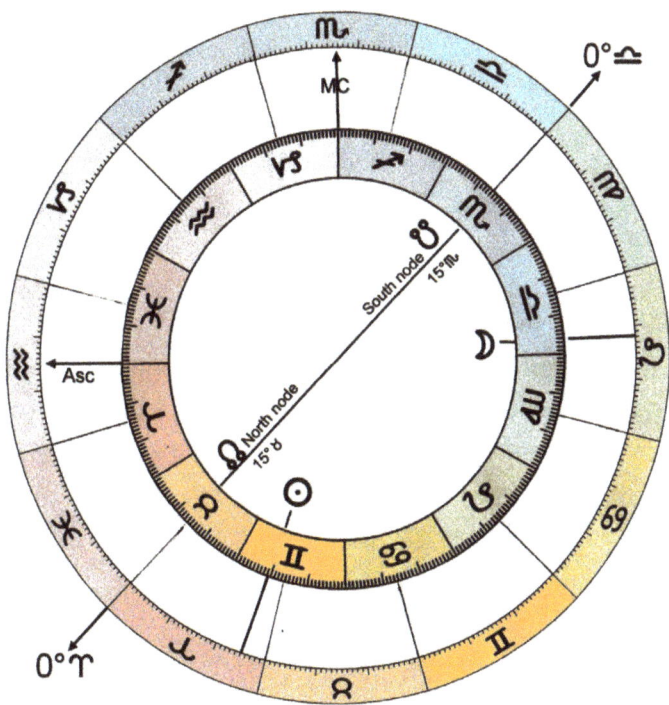

Figure 2. The tropical horoscope shown in Figure 1 is in the centre and surrounded by the draconic zodiac. Note: the north node in the draconic horoscope is at 00° 00′ Aries and aligned with the north node of the Moon in the tropical horoscope at 15° 00′ Taurus.

Interpretation of this example
As the tropical ascendant is at 0° Aries, this person could be direct, dynamic, courageous and enterprising. With the Sun in Gemini in the tropical horoscope, the person could like to interact with many different people and connect different facts. They might know something about a wide range of topics. It is likely that, with the Moon in Libra, the person would feel comfortable when there is accord and agreement in their surroundings and seeks harmony in their relationships.

In the draconic horoscope, the ascendant is at 15° Aquarius, the Sun at 25° Aries and the Moon at 18° Leo. As the emphasis has moved from Aries, Gemini and Libra in the tropical horoscope to Aquarius, Aries and Leo in the draconic horoscope, there is a completely different energy even though only one angle and two planets have been considered. The interpretations of these positions by planet and sign are covered in detail in Chapters 3 and 4 respectively.

Example 2
In another theoretical example, the same ascendant and positions of the Sun and Moon in the tropical horoscope of Example 1 are used. However, in Example 2 (Figure 3) the north node of the Moon is at 20° Gemini and the south node is at 20° Sagittarius.

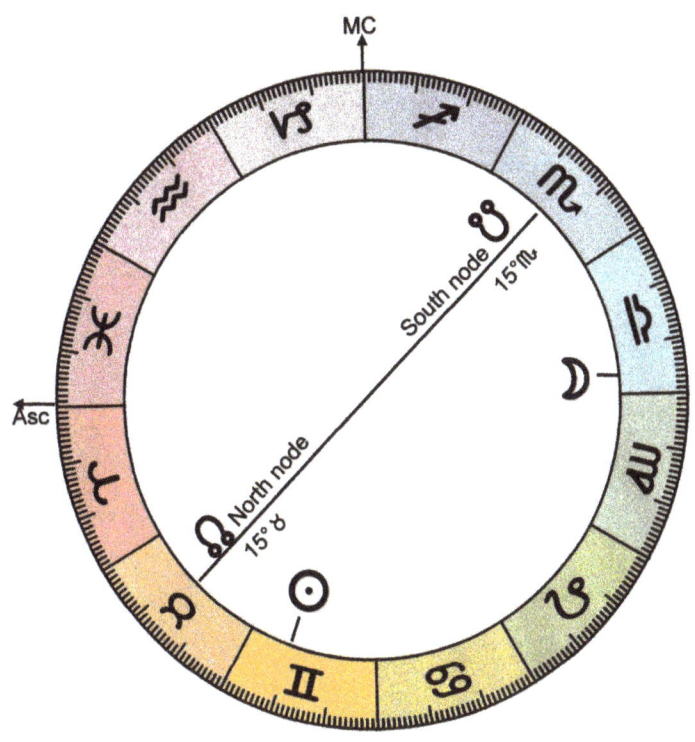

Figure 3. The tropical horoscope showing the positions of the Sun and Moon as well as the north node of the Moon at 20° 00´ Gemini and the south node of the Moon at 20° 00´ Sagittarius.

Using the method of calculation described above, the tropical north node is 80° removed from 0° Aries. All of the planets and angles move back 80° to form the draconic chart (Figure 4).

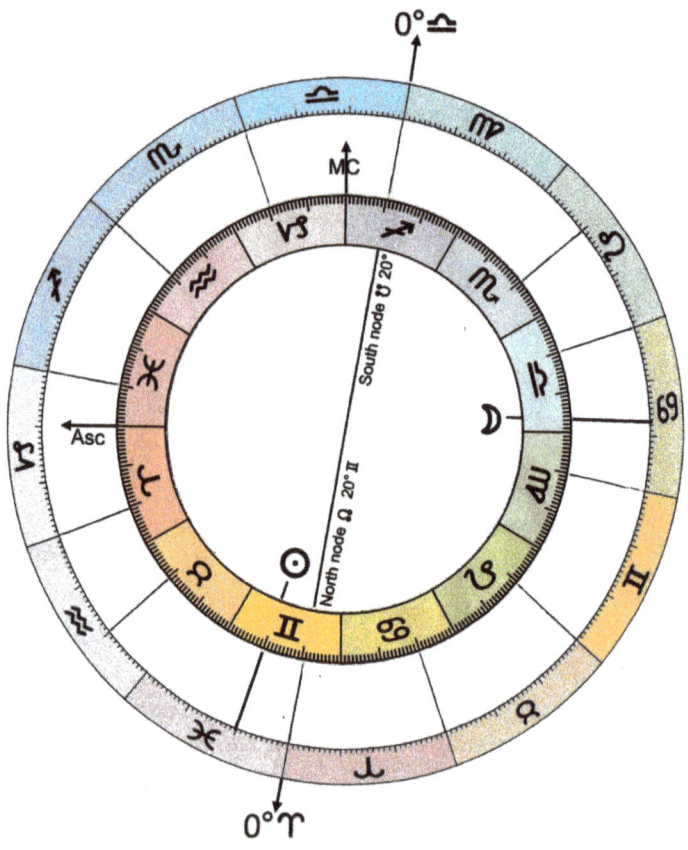

Figure 4. The tropical horoscope shown in Figure 3 is in the centre and surrounded by the draconic zodiac. Note: the north node in the draconic horoscope is at 00° 00′ Aries and aligned with the north node of the Moon in the tropical horoscope at 20° 00′ Gemini.

The draconic ascendant is at 10° Capricorn, draconic Sun at 20° Pisces and draconic Moon at 13° Cancer. There is a notable change in energies from the Aries, Gemini and Libra emphasis of the tropical horoscope to the Capricorn, Pisces and Cancer emphasis in the draconic chart. The draconic interpretations of the Sun and Moon and the signs of the zodiac are given in Chapters 3 and 4 respectively.

The theoretical Examples 1 and 2 have used the same tropical horoscope but the positions of the nodes of the Moon differ. This would not happen physically unless the Sun and Moon happened to be at the same positions of the tropical zodiac in different cycles of the nodes of the Moon many years apart. The example was used solely to demonstrate how the calculation of the draconic chart depends on the positions of the nodes of the Moon.

In both of these examples, the difference in emphasis of the signs of the zodiac between the two horoscopes is clear. There is a corresponding change in the elements and qualities of the signs occupied by the ascendant, Sun and Moon. Over and above those changes, the meditations in the next two chapters indicate that some of the interpretations of the planets and signs can be notably different between the tropical and draconic zodiacs.

Erecting a draconic horoscope by computer
When erecting a horoscope on a computer, it is useful to insert the words 'tropical' or 'draconic' after the name of the person as it helps to avoid mistakes. Although the zodiac may be specified in the list of parameters under the

person's name, these are often in small type face and easily overlooked.

The astrology software is often set up for the tropical zodiac. The choice of zodiac can usually be changed in a window giving the different zodiacs. By clicking on 'draconic', the software will compute the draconic horoscope.

Dual wheels
After erecting the tropical and draconic horoscopes by hand, it is easy to place the two horoscopes next to each other. Some astrology software does this using what may be called 'dual wheels'. The tropical and draconic horoscopes are shown side by side on the screen. The two horoscopes can now be compared, particularly noting the signs each planet occupies, the signs on the angles and on the house cusps. Much can be gained by looking at these differences.

Bi-wheels
A bi-wheel, in which one horoscope is placed around another, can be produced either by hand or using astrology software. This allows examination of aspects between planets and angles across the two horoscopes. By placing the draconic chart in the outer wheel around the tropical chart, it is possible to see how the soul's impulses are guiding the physical life. It is also possible to place the tropical horoscope around the draconic one. This is another way of studying how the soul's impulses are manifesting in the outer life. There may be the option to 'Swap' the positions of the horoscopes in some astrology software.

Looking at the interaction between the tropical and draconic charts in this way, it is possible to help a person understand him- or herself better. By recognising inner impulses and objectives, appreciating what the soul may be wanting to learn and the path taken to that end, challenges can become more comprehensible and looked at as opportunities for growth rather than difficulties and hardships. Realising and acknowledging how some of the deeper purposes of the soul are working out in everyday life can help a person work with them rather than struggle against them. Appreciating that there is a more profound reason and deeper meaning behind the events in life can help the person cope with what is going on.

General considerations
When the tropical north node is close to 0° Aries, there is little difference between the tropical and draconic charts. However, if the difference is more than a few degrees, some or all of the planets and angles can move signs. In this case, the planet(s) and angle(s) can be in one sign in the tropical horoscope and a different sign in the draconic horoscope. In other words, there is one type of energy at the physical level and another type of energy at the soul level. This is fundamental in trying to understanding the outworking of each planet at the different levels of life. It is discussed more in the last chapter of the book.

Similarly with house cusps, each house could have one sign on the cusp in the tropical horoscope but another sign on the draconic house cusp. This would mean that there were different rulers of the house cusps. The energy of the houses would be different at the soul and outer levels of manifestation.

Similarities and differences between tropical and draconic charts

There are similarities but there may also be differences between the tropical and draconic horoscopes.

Similarities
1. The planets are always in the same houses in the tropical and draconic zodiacs.
2. The planet–house association remains the same. For instance, Taurus, ruled by Venus, is associated with the second house even though a different sign on the cusp of that house would mean that there was a different house ruler.
3. The aspects between the planets stay the same.
4. The midpoints remain the same.

Differences
1. The signs of the zodiac occupied by planets and on the house cusps may be different, depending on the number of degrees that separate the tropical north node from 0° Aries.
2. If the signs of the planets are different, the planets could move into or out of dignity, detriment, exaltation and fall.
3. The relative importance of planets that is associated with the signs of the zodiac on the angles and the signs occupied by the Sun and Moon could differ between the tropical and draconic horoscopes.

The interpretations of the planets and signs garnered from meditations are described in the following chapters.

Chapter 2

Going into Meditation

Meditation can be helpful when wanting to understand life at a deeper level. Each person develops their own way of meditating. For me it is helpful to sit quietly at a time when I am unlikely to be disturbed. I try to quieten my thoughts of everyday activities. I attune myself to a higher, finer energy that is all light, love and wisdom, harmony and peace. In this way, I feel open to inspiration. I am not sure what the source of this inspiration is. It may be from my higher self. It may be from a guide. It may be from something outside of my soul and spirit: a Being or energy vibration that is beyond my comprehension. It may be from a mixture of these sources and I trust that they are working together for good. I am deeply grateful for the experiences during meditation.

When meditating on the planets and signs of the zodiac at the draconic level, I silently ask for guidance to understand them more deeply but do not specify a planet or sign to focus on. I let that unfold during the course of the meditation. During the first of the meditations, I was taken high up in the mountains where the air was pure and all was quiet. It was easier here to silence my outer mind. I was then taken into a cave that turned out to be the starting place for most of the subsequent meditations. The cave may indicate that still place within my being that can access the finer realms of life. It may also indicate a deeper level of consciousness.

There are often Beings of light present in the cave as I enter. Sometimes these Beings are what I call White Brethren or Brothers. At other times there are other Beings present. All of these Beings are of light and of a much finer energy than the physical level of life.

As I go deeper into the meditations, I become aware of the planet or sign of the zodiac that is being revealed. After the end of the meditations and while still in their peaceful energy, I write notes on my experiences. These, together with further thoughts from times of contemplation following the meditations, led to the descriptions given in the following two chapters.

I only meditated on one planet or sign each a day. In the weeks and months that followed the meditations, I tried to capture what I had experienced by painting what I had 'seen'. This was not easy as the meditations were of light and felt non-dimensional, yet I was trying to capture them in physical paints on a two-dimensional piece of paper. I wanted to paint pictures as they can portray so much more than words alone. Neither words nor pictures can completely record these inner experiences but they are the best I can do to try to pass on this information. I hope they inspire others to look for the deeper meanings of the draconic planets and signs in their own way.

For each planet and sign, there is a keyword summary of the essence of the experiences of the meditation. The comments attempt to encapsulate the differences between the tropical and draconic interpretations of the planets and signs.

I would like to point out that these are my experiences. I recognise that other people could have totally different experiences and believe that, whatever those experiences may be, they would be the right ones for that person.

The cave
This is a summary of experiences on first entering the cave on different days.

I go up a mountain that feels as if it is in the Himalayas. There is a tunnel off to the right and this leads into a cave. The cave is dark but the walls are implanted with crystals. Crystals that appear on different days of the meditations include:

- A long, thin, round cross-section, aquamarine-coloured crystal that goes through the roof of the cave. This crystal divides in two.
- A diamond-shaped, brownish amethyst crystal that is also a bit like ametrine.
- A spherical, deep red crystal goes to a planet or an unseen planet.
- A rectangular, spring green crystal.
- A yellow crystal.
- A black hole, like a gap in the ceiling, next to a blue crystal.
- A blue light in the floor.
- A ball of red light at the far end of cave.

Each crystal feels like a lens or tube through which I can pass. The crystals sometimes lead to a planet but most often to a sign of the zodiac. I believe that crystals are living beings of a fine energy that have taken the physical form of crystals. As such, seeing crystals in the meditations may represent accessing a finer level of energy and so signify a portal to other levels of awareness.

Above the domed ceiling of the cave is another ceiling. It is like looking at a planetarium. Here I can see the tropical meaning of the planets and meet the Brothers on the planets.

Above the tropical ceiling is another level made of light. I feel this represents the draconic level of life. It is made of light in beautiful colours. This level is open but contained. That sounds contradictory from a physical perspective but is possible within the meditations.

Above the ceiling of the draconic level is another level that is open and ethereal. I am not sure what this level is as it is beyond my current comprehension.

Picture of the cave
I have tried to represent the sum of these experiences in a multimedia picture. While it might look childlike in its simplicity, it is the nearest thing I can create with physical materials to what I experienced at a level of light. The tunnel and the cave are shown in midnight blue. Brothers present in the cave are shown in white. Buttons and pieces of ribbon are used to represent the crystals that become portals into other dimensions. The silver arch immediately over the cave represents the tropical level of astrology. The silver has not photographed very well so it looks pale grey. The golden arch represents the draconic level. Over the draconic level is white. I will now try to explain what I experience on each of these levels.

Figure 5. The cave

In the tropical level, the silver arch in the picture, I see the Brothers on the planets. I feel these are the great Beings who are the spiritual counterparts of the physical planets and made of light. They are the spirits of the planets. At times it can feel that they are like people with whom I can communicate but in a silent way in which no words are exchanged. It feels as if they are picking up what is happening on Earth through their powers to sense it. Sometimes it feels as if I am a transmitter and one of many means through which they can detect what is happening on Earth and in the Earth's vibrations. I feel they may be imparting information for the Earth through me as one of many, many other channels. I do not know on a conscious level what this information is but I feel that this is happening.

The draconic level, shown in gold in the picture, is the most beautiful colours of light. They are pale pastel colours that move and change. One colour replaces another in the vast display of gently moving light. It brings the feeling of each colour being perfect at that time and that place, although in the dimensions of the meditations there is no time or three dimensions as experienced on Earth. There is a feeling of perfection in whatever is happening, of love and wisdom that all is as it should be. When one colour is no longer appropriate, it changes to the colour that has become the right one. This brings a sense of freedom from the difficulties of Earth. What is happening at this level is more than faith. It is a knowing that everything is progressing and unfolding exactly as it should.

I do not know what the white level is but think it is a level that I am not yet advanced enough to be able to access.

The silver, tropical level diffuses into the gold, draconic level. Similarly, the gold, draconic level diffuses into the higher, and to me unknown, level. There are no clear cut-off divisions. This surprised me to begin with but the more I study astrology, the more I realise that the tropical level is much more physical for some people than others. Similarly, the draconic level can be closer to the physical level of life for some people but closer to the spiritual level for others. I feel that these differences may be due to the different stages of evolution of different souls but I am not sufficiently advanced in this lifetime to know this for sure.

The meditations on the planets or signs that follow on from being in the cave are described in the next two chapters.

Chapter 3

Meditations on the Draconic Meanings of the Planets

The meditations on the draconic meanings of the planets were done in the way described in the previous chapter. The meditations often started by going into the cave, symbolic of going into a still place in my inner being where it is easier to access the finer realms of life. The meditations, together with further thoughts from times of contemplation following the meditations, will now be described.

DRACONIC SUN

As I enter meditation and go into the cave, White Brethren greet me briefly and immediately show me lots of books. Then the roof of the cave opens up to the sky, to the Sun. All is bright light. As I go up into the Sun, I am aware of all the signs of the zodiac around it and can feel the draconic level of every sign. I am aware that the draconic signs are operating in the lives of all people.

I am watching the planets moving in a plane round the Sun, but as I do this I realise that I am looking at this from the Sun. Heliocentric astrology is astrology in which the planets are viewed from the Sun. (This is in contrast to most astrology practised today which views the positions of the planets from the Earth and is called geocentric astrology.) This view of looking at the planets from the Sun seems integrally linked to all of life. It is like a loom that weaves cloth but it is both the loom and the cloth at the same time.

I believe that when humanity becomes more aware of its part in life in the solar system, astrology will move to being heliocentrically based. Rather than being 'I' centred, we will become more 'We' centred. The terms 'I' and 'We' operate at many different levels, some of which can be described as follows:

- At one level, 'I' can mean me as a physical person in comparison to other people. This is self-centred and can be selfish.
- 'I' can also mean the planet Earth while 'We' means the universe. This is moving towards greater understanding of interrelationships in physical life.
- At yet another level, 'I' can mean physical life and 'We' could mean all levels of life in all dimensions.

Eventually, 'I' and 'We' become one. There is no separation. I feel that when humanity has reached this level of evolution it will be one with the spiritual Sun. Even heliocentric astrology will have taken on a different meaning as it will be cosmic, spiritual oneness. Words only inadequately express what can be experienced at this level of being.

The White Brethren are linked with the planets. The Brethren or great Beings of the planets are linked with the Being of the Sun. It is as if they breathe with it, know what the Being of the Sun is 'thinking' and the Being of the Sun knows what is going on for the Beings of the planets. At this level all is light, all is one, although somehow there is also individuality. It is a bit like the grains of sand on a beach being individual but part of the beach, or a drop of water being part of an ocean.

After experiencing this level of the Sun, the White Brethren bring me down to the physical level of consciousness stage by stage. It is lovely to be surrounded in their light. This feels protective so that I can take up physical life again.

Picture of draconic Sun
The Beings of the Sun and the planets are depicted as figures with a head and body clothed in light. The Being of the Sun is the golden figure in the centre. There are connections, made of light, going from the heart of the Being of the Sun to the hearts of each of the Beings of the planets. The Beings of the planets are different colours as indicated in the picture and to make it easier to recognise them the glyph of the planet is shown over each heart.

Figure 6. Draconic Sun

Summary of draconic Sun
The Sun is breathing with the Beings of the Planets.
All is light.
All is one, all is life.

Comment
In tropical astrology, the Sun is associated with spirit, the infinite and eternal part of all life. Draconic Sun also links with spirit but it feels to be at a much deeper level than can be touched in the tropical zodiac.

DRACONIC MOON
After raising my consciousness, I ask the angels of the Moon and the angel of draconic astrology to help me. While living in a physical body, I need to make a deliberate effort to contact higher levels of consciousness. I also seek the help of Beings that exist in the levels of consciousness that I aspire to contact. Gradually, I become aware of the Sun and the Moon and the energy connections between them that are known as the nodes of the Moon.

I go into the Moon and am aware of beams of light, 'pencil thin', going from the Sun to me in the centre of the Moon. The beams become wider until there is one beam going from the Sun to the Moon. The beam is 'soul information' flowing from the centre of the Sun to the Moon. It feels like an unhindered energy transfer between the Sun and the Moon. The Moon then moves along the beam of light to enter and become one with the Sun.

The Sun represents spirit and the Moon represents the soul, but at this level of awareness it feels as if they are one. The soul knows and is one with all that is spirit. Spirit knows and is one with all that is the soul. However, this is far too much for a human being in a physical body to cope with so the Moon moves out of the Sun. The soul moves out of spirit, taking with it only that amount of experience that the human being can cope with in one incarnation. The rest waits for other times, other incarnations.

The Moon moves into the sign of the draconic zodiac that best reflects that part of spirit which the soul wants to experience in this lifetime. This position indicates how the soul can gain greater experience on its path towards the perfection of spirit. This is a very small part of all that is spirit and perhaps one reason why so many incarnations are needed until all facets of spirit have been experienced by the soul.

For me, this meditation shows the connection between the Sun and the Moon, between spirit and soul. I believe it is a key part of draconic astrology.

Figure 7. Draconic Moon

Picture of draconic Moon

The Sun represents spirit and is shown by its glyph painted in gold. Golden rays from the Sun are the glory of spirit radiating into all that is in creation. The Moon represents the soul and is shown by the silver crescent. The golden rays from the Sun shine on the Moon but as the rays come out of the other side of the Moon, there are fewer of them and they are shown in silver. It is these rays, portrayed in silver, that surround and go through the human figure. The Moon has 'stepped down' the energy of the Sun. It is as if the soul has selected those parts of the spirit that are to be experienced by the human figure. All the other golden rays of the Sun will be experienced by the person in other incarnations.

Summary of draconic Moon

The soul could be conscious of all that is spirit but this would be too much for the soul of a human being to cope with in one lifetime so the Moon lets through only the amount that a person can manage. The rest waits for another time.

Comment

The tropical interpretation of the Moon includes a person's behaviours, habits and reactions as well as what helps the person feel secure. These ways of being may be linked with past soul experiences. The meditation on draconic Moon suggests that it indicates the part of spirit that the soul has chosen to experience now, in this life. Draconic Moon relates to the present life.

DRACONIC MERCURY

When I go into the cave, I am in the centre of a circle of White Brethren. The roof of the cave opens like a slit that gets bigger and becomes a circle. The roof of the cave rolls back over the side of the cave. This is a big opening in comparison to that seen in other meditations. The Brethren and I squeeze through the opening. Then the face of a fairly old man appears. He has big cheeks and is cheerful. He stretches his hand and forearm towards me. Although I can see his face, I do not know who he is but feel he must know me and he pulls me up into the sky. There are stars all around.

I am attracted and go into one small 'star' that is like a point of light. This is Mercury. Never before have I thought of Mercury as a small planet in comparison to the magnitude of the heavens or of it as a point of light. Mercury is small but it connects to all the other planets and the stars. The connections are on one plane. Although this could be a physical plane, I feel that this is a plane of consciousness.

Mercury is flashing like a lighthouse and I am aware that when it flashes, light and information are going out to the stars, planets and everything else on that plane. When it is not flashing, it is receiving information. This may be the time when people are not listening. The flashes and the time between the flashes are times of giving out and receiving information respectively. It could be likened to talking and listening but on a silent level of communication. In general, people on Earth like to talk and say what they think but are less prepared to listen to what other people have to say. This is not mutual, two-way communication. At this level, it feels as if Mercury is closer to the physical plane of life.

I then go to a higher level and at this level the sending out and receiving of 'information' is simultaneous and continuous with everything. It is a constant knowing of what is happening. The word 'knowing' implies intelligence and the information exchange is beyond intelligence. The 'knowing' in the meditation is a continuous and perpetual interchange that is independent of time and direction. At this level all is light. It feels as if this is the mind of the Creator, Source, God or whatever term implies the being that has created all life. It has no boundaries, is all-encompassing and all-knowing. The mind of this Source always knows what is happening with and in everything all of the time. Draconic Mercury represents when the soul is approaching the mind of this Source of life.

When it is time to return to the earthly level of consciousness, I am taken back to the flashing lighthouse as this is closer to the level of humankind and how their minds work. I go back through the roof of the cave with the White Brethren, then the roof closes to a slit. The thin opening is the limited 'gap' through which I have connection to the mind of a much higher level of consciousness. I am brought down to the floor of the cave and then back down to Earth. I am so thankful for this experience.

Figure 8. Draconic Mercury

Picture of draconic Mercury

This picture depicts the lower level of draconic Mercury seen as the flashing lighthouse in the meditation. The glyph of Mercury is painted in silver in the central circle. This circle is surrounded by concentric circles of white and blue. In the white circles golden arrows radiate outwards. These represent the times when information streams out from the centre to humanity. The blue circles are the quiet times when information is not streaming out. These are times when information can go from humanity in towards the centre. Silver arrows show the direction of flow of this information. Note that the gold and silver arrows do not meet but are staggered. This represents how people cannot talk and truly listen at the same time.

A picture of the higher level of draconic Mercury might be all pale blue with golden arrows going from the centre to the outside of the picture side by side with silver arrows going from the outside to the centre.

Summary of draconic Mercury

Mercury is like a flashing lighthouse, sending out information when it is flashing, receiving information when it is not flashing.
All information, in and out, is continuous with everything.
Mercury is linked with the mind of Source, the Creator, God. The mind of God always knows what is happening with everything.
All-light, all-knowledge, all-knowing.

Comment

Tropical Mercury indicates the mind, how a person thinks and communicates. The principles of draconic Mercury are similar but elevated beyond conscious thought and the physical level of life, suggesting that the soul may be aware of a level of 'mind' that is beyond the limitations of the human intellect.

DRACONIC VENUS

On entering meditation, I feel that I am near or in Venus, and I have to ask if this is so. It feels as if I am asking to make a more conscious connection with the planet. For me this is confirmed when I see five Brethren standing in the shape of a pentacle. This is similar to the pattern Venus makes in the heavens, when viewed from the Earth, during its five retrograde phases, which take eight years to complete. It is a beautiful pattern that resembles a rose with five petals.

A sixth Brother is in the centre. This Brother moves to the circle and another Brother takes its place, making six petals of a rose or six points of a star plus one in the centre. The central point may represent the Source of all creation, the Creator, God. Another way of looking at this is that the six outer points plus the central one make seven, which could represent the Seven Rays. It feels right for me to stay with this configuration. However, I am aware that the movement of the Brother in the centre to the outside with another Brother appearing in the centre could go on ad infinitum. This brings the feeling of the continuous stream of God's love flowing to creation.

I become aware that Venus steps down the infinite love of God to the amount that humans on Earth can cope with. This is comparable to the way the draconic level of the Moon steps down and selects the part of spirit that a person can manage in one incarnation. In the case of Venus, it feels as if the planet is not selecting but simply reducing how much of the love of God gets through to the person. As the love and wisdom of God is all-power, most humans could not cope with this. Their physical bodies would 'blow a fuse'. I think of Uranus as it is the planet associated with electricity. Uranus is also linked with truth and light; the truth of the magnitude and glory of the infinite wisdom and unconditional love of God that is all-powerful. This is like the expression 'white-out', which implies that nothing can be seen because there is so much white light. God is like white-out: all-encompassing, infinite love. This is too much for humans to take in one go. Venus steps it down to manageable amounts.

Various colours are seen in this meditation. The source of all the love, God, is seen as white, the white-out already mentioned. Initially, the love streaming out from God is seen as yellow/pink. This is not the individual colours but a magical blend of both of them. Venus is encircled by pink and white light but only pink is passed on to Earth. I feel that I do not fully understand the differences in these colours as they are not simply colours but energies.

Figure 9. Draconic Venus

Picture of draconic Venus

The glyph of the Sun is a dot within a circle. Part of it is shown in gold and white in the top right-hand corner. The whole glyph is often associated with spirit but in this picture it would represent God. Only part of the symbol is shown here to indicate that a human being cannot see all of God. Yellow, gold and strong pink radiating from this represent the love of God. Strong colours have been used to show how strong God's love is.

A pink circle almost in the middle of the picture represents Venus. It is not obvious at first in comparison to the strong colours. Venus is one part of God's creation. The size of the physical planet of Venus is small relative to the size of the heavens but I believe it is an integral part of life and that physical size cannot be related to the significance of this planet to the whole of life across all levels and dimensions.

A beam of pale pink goes away from Venus. There is a figure of a human being in this pale beam. The paleness of the beam represents how the amount of God's love, wisdom and power are stepped down as they are passed on to the human person. It is pale in comparison to the strength of the total love, wisdom and power of God. At the present stage of human evolution in the 21st century, most human beings can only cope with this reduced amount of love. I believe that as humanity evolves it will be able to cope with much more and will eventually move into constant and complete awareness of God. At that stage, pictures of this sort will not be needed.

Summary of draconic Venus

God is like 'white-out' – all-encompassing, infinite Love. This is too much for people on Earth to cope with. They would 'blow a fuse'. Venus reduces the amount of love to what a human can cope with at this stage of human evolution.

Comment
At the tropical level, Venus signifies beauty, harmony, love, what a person values and what brings pleasure. The draconic level of Venus indicates the part of the total love of Source that the soul is working on in the current life.

DRACONIC MARS

This meditation is unusual in that it starts with awareness of my body. Awareness of self can be linked to Aries, which is ruled by Mars. However, the awareness is far more detailed because I am conscious of every cell of my body. At the same time, I realise that every cell is receiving from and transmitting to all of the universe. This is a far wider level of consciousness. The experience is a mixture of in and out, minute and enormous. These extremes are like Scorpio, which is also ruled by Mars.

After this, I become aware of the cave and all that is in it. The wall of the cave is lined with crystals including a knobbly orange crystal that looks a bit like a knobbly exercise ball. It also reminds me of a sweet chestnut, which is covered in soft fine spines, and brings the feeling of a shell that can be removed. The shell falls off and leaves a hard, shiny ball inside. Perhaps this can be likened to the hard and prickly outer persona that people often show to the world. This persona protects the core of strength inside them. It sounds paradoxical to say that a prickly outer covering is there to protect strength.

The hard, shiny, orange ball begins to glow and orange light travels up my arms and shoulders. This light is courage and strength. Then I dissolve in the light and become one with it. The individual me is no longer visible. I am no longer physical strength with the need to protect myself but I have become one with a much higher level of courage and strength. This is the courage to do God's will and the strength to follow that will.

As I leave the physical level and merge with the higher level, the harshness of needing to maintain individuality fades away. The orange light merges with everything. Even the Sun is part of all this. At this level, all is merged, selfless and strong. There is no individuality. Consideration is from an all-is-one perspective. All is one power: the power and strength of God. It is easier to be one with all that is and the orange colour softens into a peachy colour accordingly. This is strength and power in ways not recognised on Earth.

On Earth, strength and power have often been used by one person or nation over other another person, people or nations. At the higher level, strength and power simply are. They are part of the oneness of all life; qualities of spirit that the soul is learning to use in a way that is for the highest good of all concerned. Draconic Mars is the strength and courage to act for the good of all rather than individual benefit.

'Consideration' is a word rarely associated with Mars. It is more related to Libra. Libra is the sign in which Mars is in detriment. However, the draconic level of Mars includes this very quality. Draconic Mars is courage, strength, power and consideration all blended together.

Figure 10. Draconic Mars

Picture of draconic Mars
The golden circle with the strong orange colour inside it represents the hard ball of orange in the meditation and the need of the physical being to be strong and protect itself. Going away from the golden circle, the orange colour softens. What humans think of as strength is not really strength but more of a need to look after themselves and assert their individuality. As soon as we get away from these apparent needs, there is all-encompassing love and strength, which is shown by the peachy colours in the rest of the picture.

Another way of looking at this picture is that the strength of God is at the centre of all life and that this is represented by the strong orange colour within the golden circle. All that is outside of that does not have the same strength. This shows that when we can be at one with God, our power is limitless but then it is directed by infinite love and infinite wisdom.

These completely different ways of interpreting what, at a physical level, is a very simple picture show the paradoxes contained in life.

Summary of draconic Mars
The Light is courage and strength.
It merges with everything.
It is the power and strength of God.
All is merged, selfless, strong, no individuality, considerate from an all-is-one perspective.
All is one power.

Comment
There are similarities between tropical and draconic Mars regarding courage and strength. However, at the draconic

level, this is for the good of all rather than for pursuing personal desires and urges associated with tropical Mars.

DRACONIC JUPITER

To begin with, three Masters stand in a triangle. A Being I call the Golden One is within the triangle of the Masters. This is a simple image but brings up the deeper meanings of the numbers of three and four or three plus a central One. This does not feel very clear, which may mean that I am seeing things which are at the limits of my state of consciousness. I am experiencing more at a level that is outside physical consciousness. I feel now that it is profound and has an effect across levels and dimensions of my being beyond my physical body.

A circle forms of the Masters and Brethren. The Golden One is present but I am not sure if it is part of the circle. Within the circle a *fleur-de-lis* forms and this again brings up the significance of the number three. It is difficult to interpret this symbol without the connotations connected with some religions. I feel that it can represent the unity with or separation from the divinity within life. The *fleur-de-lis* changes into a fountain that gushes up and up but it is not of water. It is made of light. It goes up so far that it feels like the top of a mountain. It is very close to the Sun. It feels as if Jupiter may work with the Sun.

Although the image of a fountain implies movement, at this highest level of the 'fountain' everything is still and silent. The stillness of inner truth, of openness. Here there is all-knowledge, all-wisdom. In this state of consciousness, everything is known by everything else so there is complete truth and honesty. Everything is open to be seen by everything else. This state of all-knowing feels completely still because there is no direction or movement to find out anything. It sounds paradoxical but this all-knowing feels like nothing, no thing, because it is everything. It is far more than 'all at once' because it is outside of time.

This profound level of knowing is the draconic level of Jupiter. It is when knowledge goes far beyond the earthly level of knowledge and understanding. There is a link between this limitless knowledge and the infinite wisdom of spirit. As spirit is represented by the Sun in astrology, this level of Jupiter can be linked with the Sun. The word 'knowledge' is associated with facts that can be learned while wisdom comes through experience of life, including learnable facts.

I believe that there is no limit to wisdom. What humans perceive as limit is more determined by the stage of evolution. I am unable to know how much humanity can evolve as this is beyond my physical level of comprehension. However, at an inner level when in higher states of consciousness, I feel that we can expand to be in the state of all-knowing and all-wisdom. In order to reach these levels, we also need to practise infinite love. As I write this, it feels that wisdom and love are infinite.

At the end of the meditation, rectangular plates of silver, like thick silver paper, are put round me. These layers form protection as I come down from this level of consciousness and back into the cave.

I thank the Beings for protecting me after the profound experience of this meditation.

Figure 11. Draconic Jupiter

Picture of draconic Jupiter

The pale blue background is the presence of all that is, all-wisdom at all levels and in all dimensions of creation. At the bottom of the fountain, darker blue streams represent the expansion of one level of knowledge. As this rises and becomes finer, higher levels of knowledge and wisdom become more obvious and these are represented by the white parts of the fountain. Intermingled with these parts are fine streaks of silver, which have not photographed well. These are hardly visible just as the highest levels of wisdom are harder to access. The ever-rising fountain represents ever-expanding wisdom and consciousness.

Summary of draconic Jupiter

Up and up to the top of a fountain, close to the Sun.
Very still.
The stillness of inner truth.
Nothing – but this is profound.

Comment

Tropical Jupiter relates to opportunities, expansion, self-improvement and trust in life. At the draconic level, this planet represents how the soul is striving for infinite wisdom and truth.

DRACONIC SATURN

This meditation opens with what appears to be a gemstone that has been cut in one of the traditional cuts. There is a flat upper surface surrounded by facets and the underside of the gemstone is pointed. The jewel in this meditation is upside down so the point is uppermost. The jewel opens as the facets of the point separate, a bit like the petals of a flower bud separating as it opens to a full bloom. The whole jewel begins to radiate light that softens the edges of its facets. It becomes like a rose made of light and I wonder if it represents Venus or if Venus is linked to this meditation. The whole thing becomes a ball of radiant deep pink light.

Karma goes into the ball of pink light and the resolution to the karma becomes apparent. Solutions to how to heal or make amends for previous past deeds come out of the centre of the light. This shows how love can heal all situations, all misdemeanours and all that is not of love.

I go into the pink ball of light and love. There are large Beings wearing dull amethyst-coloured robes. The dull colour gives the impression of the seriousness of the situation. I feel these are the Lords of Karma. The circle opens up and in the centre is a small Being of pure white light. This Being is perfect and I feel that I am not good enough. I am aware of the many things that I have done wrong in this life, some of which I know about but also others that I have not considered to be wrong but which go against the principles of unconditional love. I feel the central Being knows what I have done. However, the only criticism is from me. There is no judgement from the Being, only deep understanding. Somehow, I am able to go towards the Being and merge with it. It seems the only thing to do: to face up to what I have done. 'Things' happen in that state although I do not consciously know what they are. I feel I am filled with love and wisdom so that as I emerge from that Being I know what I have to do to resolve previous misdoings. The circle of the Lords of Karma opens to let me out so that I can go and do what I have to do.

I feel this meditation links with the draconic level of Saturn as Saturn is linked with the past and karma. It is the planet that teaches us what we need to know most. By going into the pure white and perfect central Being, I am able to see where I am not perfect. This is largely about what I have done wrong in the past rather than what I still have to learn in the future. I cannot remember the deep and profound experience of being merged with the central Being. Deep soul experiences can be like this. I know something has happened but I do not know what. I feel this meditation helped me to contact my soul's longings to correct and learn from my past. This is what draconic Saturn shows in a horoscope.

The connection to Venus could be on several different levels. At one level, Saturn is in exaltation in Libra, which is ruled by Venus. At another level, the profound love of the Source of all creation, the Creator, God, is infinite love as described in the meditation on Venus. This infinite love allows for resolving past karma.

Figure 12. Draconic Saturn

Picture of draconic Saturn
In the top left-hand corner of the picture is a representation of the jewel after the point has opened up like the petals of a flower. The black blob moves from outside the jewel into the centre of the open pink crystal. Here it is transformed into a deep pink open rose as the solution to previous misdoings is found. The rose moves out of the open crystal as these solutions are put into practice in everyday life.

The circle of amethyst-robed Beings in the main part of the picture represents the Lords of Karma. In the centre, the figure painted in radiant cream represents the pure white and perfect Being. It feels as if this is the centre from which the ultimate solutions come but the Lords of Karma are integrally involved. In some way the Lords of Karma are shielding the pure white Being. There are eighteen figures representing the Lords of Karma. I did not paint a specific number but this is the number that formed. 18 = 3 x 6, 6 = 2 x 3. 18 = 2 x 9. 9 = 3 x 3. There are so many permutations of the number three in the number eighteen that I feel it is significant at many different levels but have not looked any deeper into it yet.

Summary of draconic Saturn
A jewel opens to form a rose. Karma goes into the centre and the solution comes out.
The Lords of Karma around a white Being. It is possible to go to that Being to find out how to resolve previous conditions.

Comment
Tropical Saturn relates to restrictions and limitations that teach a person what he or she most needs to learn. The

above description of draconic Saturn suggests that the soul chooses what it needs to work on in this lifetime.

DRACONIC URANUS
I had seen the Brothers on the day before this meditation and, unlike the robes of white light that I normally see, there were flashes of colour in their robes. The Brothers are already present as I approach the entrance of the tunnel that leads to the cave. They are gently laughing. This is in contrast to their usual stillness. On entering the cave, more Brothers are present and gently laughing. These two differences – the coloured flashes in the robes and the gentle laughing of the Brothers – lead me to think about Uranus. I go to the centre of the circle of Brothers and, unusually, I ask to see draconic Uranus.

The walls of the cave are lined with crystals and today there are beams of light between the crystals. These beams form the shape of a Star of David with different colours on each side. The colours are red, blue, green, yellow, violet and orange. Over the course of the meditation, these colours become stronger at one end of each colour and paler towards the other end. At this level the Star represents the physical level of life; it shows the many colours or facets of earthly life and how each facet is stronger in some circumstances than others. It can also represent how each facet of physical life comes into being, grows and has its pinnacle of existence then fades as something else takes over.

Inside the coloured star is a silver star and I feel that this is the soul level of being. Inside the silver star is a blazing star of white light. This level is draconic Uranus. It is the truth of God, which is fine and powerful. It is so fine and powerful that humans at present can't cope with it, process it or use it so it is stepped down to the silver star that the human soul can use.

These different levels raise the fundamental question that originally led me to meditate on the draconic expression of the planets and signs of the zodiac. Is draconic astrology the soul level of astrology, a spiritual level or something else that is beyond my comprehension? Even with much subsequent contemplation on this, I am still not sure what level of life draconic Uranus corresponds to.

I feel that this uncertainty with regard to the significance of the draconic level of Uranus may apply to the draconic level of the other planets. My current thoughts are that for young souls with little experience, the draconic level is close to the physical level. For more experienced souls, draconic astrology may involve finer vibrations and be moving towards the spiritual level. Some souls may be so advanced that they are approaching the spiritual level of being. Draconic astrology may well be the soul's impulses but these may range from nearly physical to those of spirit.

In this meditation, the need to step down the fine and powerful qualities of a higher power that governs all life to those that humans can cope with and use is similar to experiences in meditations on draconic Moon and draconic Venus. In the case of Uranus, it is the purity, truth, power, love and wisdom of the Source, Creator, God, that has to be stepped down to what the soul and human being can manage.

While still in the mediation, I ask to go to draconic Uranus. As this is the second request, I seem to be persistent in this meditation. The draconic Being of Uranus puts out arms that appear to be made of light. I reach up to this Being and gradually merge into Uranus and then into the heart of it. Here, at one level, I understand the truth and power of a supreme Being but know that I am only experiencing what I can access at my current stage of evolution. There is far more that is beyond my reach. Eventually, I withdraw from this Being, from the hands of Uranus, and back into the cave and then my physical body. I thank Uranus for letting me experience this meditation. This, like many of the other meditations, is a profound experience.

Picture of draconic Uranus
The different levels of Uranus are shown in this picture. On the outside are coloured lines that represent different facets of physical life. They do not fade towards one end as described in the meditation.

Inside the coloured star is a star of silver and this represents the soul level. Inside this is a white star that represents the draconic level of Uranus, the truth and purity of God. However, every time I look at this picture I feel different things. It is dynamic and changes. Sometimes, the silver part represents draconic Uranus and the white star is something higher. In the very centre is a tiny dot formed where I placed the point of a compass on the paper during the construction of the picture. This dot, although not intentionally part of the picture, feels as if it represents something that is almost beyond what I can reach. Perhaps the dot represents God. It is the centre of everything.

The dynamic nature of this picture may reflect how the levels of consciousness I can access differ on different days. It may also represent how draconic astrology and draconic Uranus manifest in different ways at different stages of soul evolution.

Figure 13. Draconic Uranus

Summary of draconic Uranus
The coloured star is physical life.
The silver star is the soul.
The white star in the centre is draconic Uranus, the truth of God: purity, power, infinite love, wisdom.
This is so fine and powerful that it is beyond what humans can process so it is stepped down by the silver star to what we can use.

Comment
At the tropical level, Uranus indicates sudden and unexpected events, originality and humanitarian ideals, all of which bring a person closer to his or her inner truth. The position of draconic Uranus indicates that part of the absolute truth of Source that the soul wants to approach in the current life.

DRACONIC NEPTUNE
This meditation is like looking at a big sheet of paper through a pane of glass or clear plastic. There is nothing blocking the view of the piece of paper but I can only see it when there is no reflection from the glass/plastic. Some of the time, I can see a reflection of myself or my surroundings in the glass/plastic. At these times, I cannot see the paper or can only see some areas of the paper through the glass/plastic.

I think this represents humans when they are so absorbed with themselves that they look for material things related to the physical self and the physical level of life. At such times, they only see the illusion of the physical self: their reflection or a part of their reflection from the clear glass or plastic. This leads to muddle and confusion about what is real and what is not real. When people have clear vision, they are able to see through this illusion, through the glass/plastic, to what lies beyond it. This can be the higher worlds, spirit and towards God.

At the draconic level of Neptune, we transcend all illusion and everything that apparently separates us from God. We transcend all boundaries known in the physical world, including the physical body, and are aware of our soul and spirit. I believe that, depending on our stage of evolution, draconic Neptune can help us to become conscious of our soul, the impulses it receives from spirit, or even direct spiritual impulses.

Figure 14. Draconic Neptune

Picture of draconic Neptune
This is actually not a picture but a model of what was experienced in the meditation. A clear film has been placed over a sheet of plain white paper and was difficult to photograph. The reflecting film represents how humans see life. The paper represents the higher worlds and leading to God. By holding the 'picture' up and looking at it, one can see reflections of the physical self and the surroundings. By moving the 'picture' so that the light falls on it in a different way, one can see through the plastic and then get a clear view of the sheet of paper. This represents looking through the illusion of physical life to see what is real: life beyond the boundaries of illusion.

Summary of draconic Neptune
We can look at the illusion of physical life or see through that into higher worlds, spirit and towards God.
Draconic Neptune represents transcending all boundaries between the different levels of life so we are one with all that is, one with God.

Comment
Tropical Neptune is linked with illusion, imagination, impermanence and transcending boundaries. Draconic Neptune indicates the soul striving to see through the illusion of physical life and transcend this limitation to become one with the infinite and eternal Source, with God.

DRACONIC PLUTO
This is another apparently very simple meditation that is very deep and profound. As I enter the meditation, I am only aware of perfection. I am conscious of a 'blueprint' of the

perfection and that I am striving to reach that perfection. Experiences on Earth contribute to what needs to be learned in order to reach that state. Perfection is absolute stillness but this is a dynamic state as it is continuously evolving. If something moves out of the state of perfection, a subtle change occurs so as to realign to perfection again.

In this state of absolute stillness and perfection, I am aware of the power of spirit and the spirit of power. All is integrally linked with Love and Wisdom. Spirit, power, love and wisdom are life, the power of and in life. There is a connection at this level with the Sun. As the Sun is at the centre of the solar system and Pluto is the outermost known planet, they are linked like the beginning and the end, the centre and the outside, the Alpha and the Omega.

Draconic Pluto is the power of spirit used with unconditional love and infinite wisdom. This power is far stronger and infinitely more widely reaching than what humans think of as power on Earth. Even the strongest human power, in any sense of the word, is only a part of the power of Source, Creator, God, that humans are allowed to use. It is nothing compared to the power of that infinite Source.

Figure 15. Draconic Pluto

Picture of draconic Pluto
The only way that I could portray the many deep meanings of the meditation was to paint a silver circle surrounded by gold. The gold surrounding the silver brings a feeling of the infinite power of spirit. Although there is a feeling that the silver circle is spirit, it is encompassed by a much stronger power so this could be taking the meaning of draconic Pluto to an even deeper level. The simplicity of this picture brings the feeling of dynamic stillness experienced in the meditation.

Summary of draconic Pluto
The dynamic stillness of maintaining perfection as it evolves. The spirit of power, the power of Spirit.

Comment
Tropical Pluto is associated with change and transformation, beginnings and endings. These can be traumatic at the physical level of manifestation. Tropical Pluto can also relate to power. At the draconic level, there is absolute stillness within evolving perfection. Draconic Pluto indicates how the soul is striving to reach the power associated with the love and wisdom of Source, of God.

Chapter 4

Meditations on the Draconic Meanings of the Signs of the Zodiac

On the days when I wanted to meditate on the draconic meanings of the signs of the zodiac, I went into meditation, arrived at the cave, then was drawn to a crystal and went through it. The meditation unfolded and at some point I realised which sign the meditation was on. They were not in the order of the zodiac but I have arranged them in that order for ease of reference.

DRACONIC ARIES

This is like a pure white light that is Source and radiates clearly and with a sense of purpose. It is an impulse of Spirit, of Source, the Creator, God. It is simplicity, purity, a simple and pure impulse. It is God in action, the direction of God being taken out into life.

This is like the description given in some books of the first sign of the zodiac being the impulse of a soul to leave the light in order to experience duality and life on Earth. It is a very simple meditation.

Figure 16. Draconic Aries

Picture of draconic Aries

This picture may seem to be contrary to what has just been written. The pale yellow background represents the golden light of God. The arrow is the strong, direct impulse to get back to Spirit or God, which is represented by the golden circle. The simple sense of purpose is clear.

Summary of draconic Aries

The pure impulse to reach God.
Single-pointed direction.

Comments

Tropical Aries is linked with direct action, shows initiative and is enterprising. Draconic Aries is the single-pointed impulse towards the Source of all life, towards God. This is a deeper and more profound focus that surpasses any goals of the personality.

DRACONIC TAURUS

I go along the tunnel into the cave where I am greeted by White Brothers. There is a sky blue opening in the floor and I go through it into the sky. I am looking at a very earthly image of tiles on roofs, lots of roofs with lovely tiles of many shades of reds and browns. This is puzzling and I feel that I am going in the wrong direction. I look into the substance of the tiles, which are made of fired earth.

Then the roofs turn upside down and are open to the sky, there is a sense of release and I can fly up and up and not worry about physical things any more. I go into the home of God, into the Sun and Light. Here there is no possession and no ownership because everything is of God. There is Light, such beauty, and this comes through the absence of ownership as is known in earthly life. God is in everything so everything is part of God. This feels like perfect brotherhood and links with the eleventh house.

Seeing the tiles made of earth and the sense of no ownership leads me to realise that this meditation is on draconic Taurus. This earth sign can be linked with building on Earth. Furthermore, there is a facet of Taurus that likes to possess and own physical objects as these can bring a sense of material security in some cases. The absence of the need to own things in the meditation brings a sense of freedom. It frees humanity from the feeling that 'I have this thing so I am safe'.

As both the eleventh house and Taurus have come up in this meditation, it feels as if Taurus at the draconic level links with the eleventh house. More inner work is needed to understand this.

The light and freedom in this meditation bring realisation that God is in all physical things, the very atoms of matter. God is light and light penetrates the Earth and all matter on Earth. All matter is of God. Draconic Taurus represents the beauty and Light of God coming to Earth, lifting the world up into Light, blending Earth and Light. There is Oneness, Beauty and Light. Light, God and building on Earth resonate at this inner level.

I come down to the cave, floating on a feather that is carried by an eagle. I come through the ceiling of the cave and sit cross-legged on the floor of the cave. The action of me coming through the ceiling of the cave brings the crystals that I have seen in the roof of the cave falling into my lap. This may signify the higher vibrations of life being crystallised as they take up physical form. I am thankful for the abundance of this meditation.

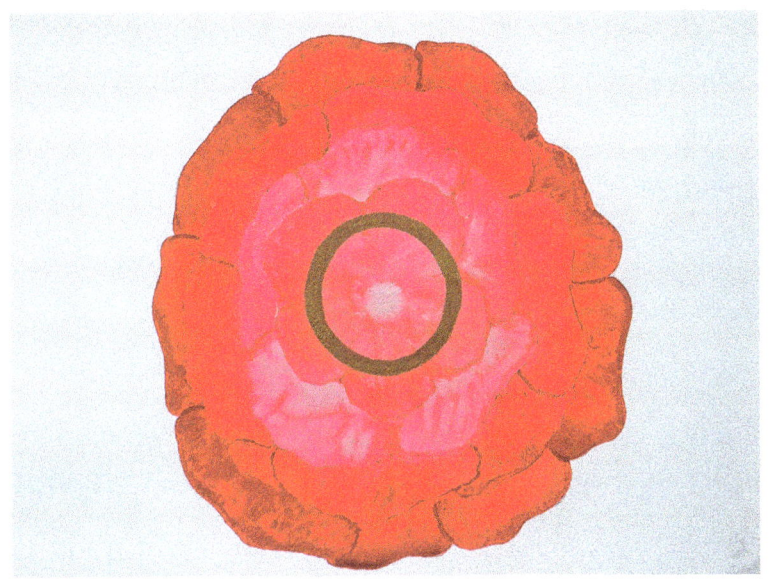

Figure 17. Draconic Taurus

Picture of draconic Taurus

The picture is of a rose and illustrates draconic Taurus. The rose symbolises the essence of life: the light, love and beauty of life. Around the edges, the rose is more solid to signify the physical level of life. Going towards the centre, the rose becomes paler to suggest it is more ethereal and made of light rather than physical substance. As the vibration of the rose becomes finer and purer, it is closer to God, represented by the circle of gold. This is a contradiction in terms as all levels of life, even the physical level, are of God.

Summary of draconic Taurus

Here there is no possession, no ownership because everything is of God.
The beauty and light of God coming to Earth.
Oneness, Beauty, Light.

Comments

Tropical Taurus is linked with consolidation and building, ownership, tangible assets and the security they appear to bring. The draconic level of Taurus relates to non-attachment and the freedom this can lead to. Tropical Taurus can be sensuous and loves beauty, particularly the beauty of nature. Draconic Taurus relates to a finer level of beauty. It is the light and beauty of God coming to Earth.

DRACONIC GEMINI

The beginning of this meditation is different from other meditations. I go to the top of a mountain and into the Sun and then down into the cave.

There is a long, thin, round cross-sectioned, aquamarine-coloured crystal that goes through the roof. I feel that the crystal leads to Mercury and divides to go to Gemini and Virgo, the two signs ruled by Mercury. Later on in this series of meditations another crystal leads to Virgo and I am shown that the second limb of the aquamarine-coloured crystal leads to Libra. Although Gemini and Virgo are both ruled by Mercury, Gemini and Libra are both air signs and they both have two parts to their symbols. In the case of Gemini it is the twins and with Libra it is the two pans on the scales. Gemini and Libra are also both involved with connections: Gemini through connecting information and Libra through balancing and harmonising the different sides of anything. There is an understanding of two-ness in both of these signs so it fits with the crystal leading from the roof dividing in two.

The limb of the crystal that leads to Gemini is about connecting the human mind to the mind of God.

There is a head with antennae sensing information in the environment. The antennae become tubes, conduits, for bubbles that represent small defined particles of God mind. These small amounts of the mind of God are let out into the world but only to the extent that humanity can deal with at this stage of its evolution. Information is going out from the mind of God to the world.

I can look down from the particles of God mind to Mercury. When I look up, I go into the Source of Light. There is an emanation of light from this Source. There is a sense of a higher, finer vibration, of Light, of the unbounded mind of God that far exceeds anything my human mind can comprehend. God mind is absolute stillness. Draconic Gemini is the emanation of the God mind, God intellect, knowledge coming from God to Earth.

There seem to be three levels of contact that I can feel with draconic Gemini. There is contact at the level of mind as described above. Another level feels as if there is contact at a soul level, the heart of one soul to the heart of another soul. The third level of contact feels quite physical, like skin.

The overall impression by the end of this meditation is that of oneness of the God mind with all creation. At this level there is no need to connect to or to communicate with anything because all is one. As the business of connecting things no longer exists, there is absolute stillness.

Picture of draconic Gemini
The coloured circles around the outside of this picture represent the many facets of life that humans like to connect. Each facet of life is connected to adjacent facets and these connections are indicated by the silver lines. Each coloured circle is also connected to the golden circle around the centre just as all parts of life are connected to God. It is via God, represented by the golden circle and lines, that one area of life is connected to areas that are apparently completely removed from it. In the centre is a circle of plain white. This represents the mind of God that, due to complete oneness with everything, does not need the channels of connection used in physical life.

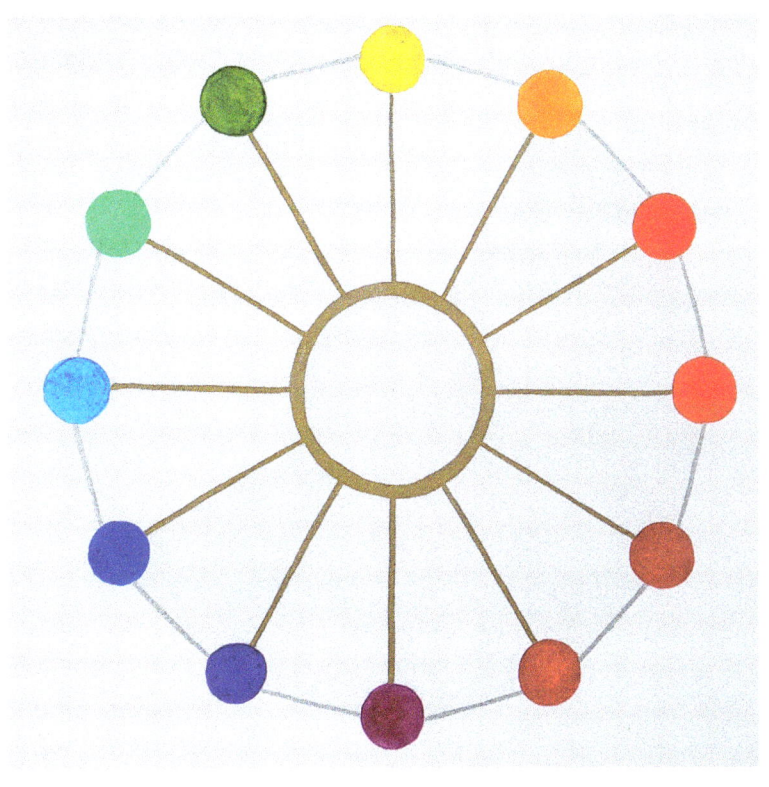

Figure 18. Draconic Gemini

Summary of draconic Gemini
The emanation of the God mind, God intellect, God knowledge, to Earth.
God mind is absolute stillness.

Comments
This meditation indicates one of the greatest differences between the draconic and tropical zodiacs. At the tropical level, Gemini is concerned with gathering many pieces of information necessitating communication, connecting things, and busy-ness. At the draconic level, there is complete stillness. This may be because at the level of the infinite mind all information is already connected so there is no need for communication. Infinite mind is all-information, all-knowledge and all-wisdom.

DRACONIC CANCER
I enter the tunnel and then the cave. The cave is filled with light and at the far end of the cave at floor level there is a 'crystal' of brilliant white light. Inside the centre of the light is absolute stillness. The words 'quiet' and 'calm' are too soft for the strength of the feeling here. I go into the crystal, into the light, and see enormous hands that are cupped and holding the world. The world is held in light.

The world is completely protected and cared for as a complete entity; as something much bigger and more whole than the individual events and happenings on the physical plane. There is a very strong sense that everything is being looked after and consequently there is absolute tranquillity, a dynamic peace that can adjust to anything that may come along and still remain calm.

At this stage, the world looks small and hard but then bursts open with light. It feels as if this is a change in consciousness and dimension. The world becomes light. This is the light that is the inner vibration of the world. Light is the God-substance of Earth. Light is what feeds and sustains life, all life including all that is on the Earth as well as the Earth itself.

This substance, God, is in the entire universe and so connects the Earth with all of creation. There is an awareness of the Beings of the Planets and the Beings in other parts of life.

This whole scene bursts open, like the world did earlier in the meditation. This happens again and again in ever higher dimensions. It goes beyond what I can comprehend. It is infinite and it is all cared for in this infinite light.

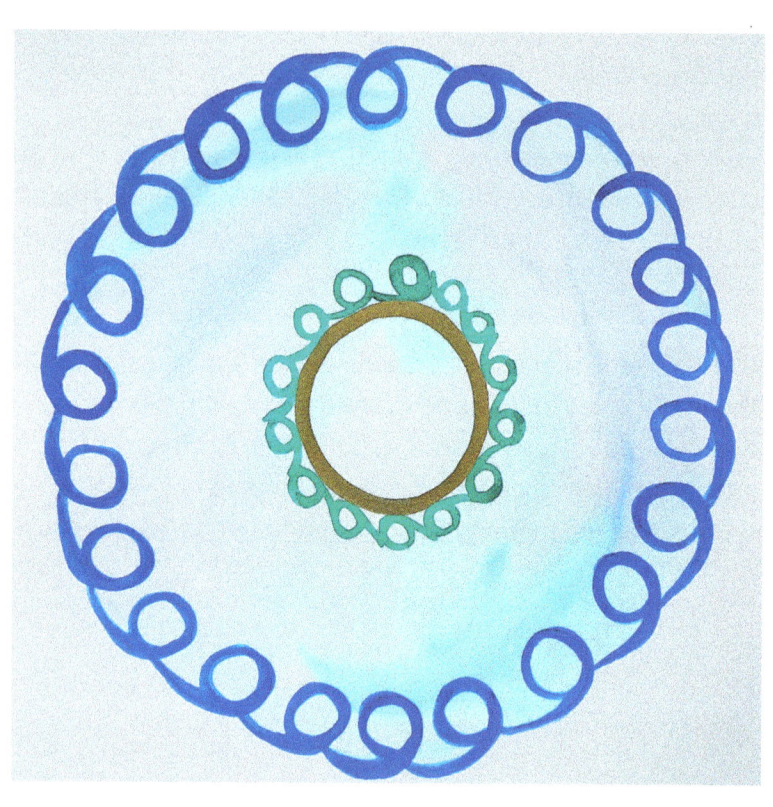

Figure 19. Draconic Cancer

Picture of draconic Cancer

The two parts of the symbol of Cancer have drawn apart and each is repeated many times to form two circles: the outer one is blue and the inner one is green. Life is cupped between these two circles so that it is enfolded, held, cared for and protected in all ways. Inside the green circle is a golden ring representing spirit, God. The infinite care of God permeates all life; both the inner life, represented by the pale green inside the gold circle, and the outer life shown as pale blue and pale green between the two parts of the symbols of Cancer.

Summary of draconic Cancer

Light is what feeds and sustains life for ever, and ever, and ever.
The structure of all life – infinite – all cared for.
Surety that all is all right.

Comments

Cancer is the sign where there is the greatest similarity between the tropical and draconic zodiacs. They are similar in their caring and nurturing qualities. The main difference is that while tropical Cancer may apply to family and known life, draconic Cancer applies to all levels of life.

DRACONIC LEO

As I go into the cave there is a small yellow star-shaped crystal in the ceiling. I go through this, initially into the darkness which represents the unknown in the space between the ceiling of the cave and the tropical ceiling. As I go up through the tropical ceiling the scene opens up into a dome of warmth and light. This suggests that the meditation is on draconic Leo as Leo is ruled by the Sun. Other qualities of Leo such as generosity, flamboyance and wanting to be seen are also experienced.

There is an expansive feeling that all is well, of total unconditional love and loving all that is. The soul lesson of Leo is love.

There is an awareness of being love and being life. Not only are love and life in every cell of a physical body but also in all that is in creation. This is life: it is everything. The expansive feeling of this experience goes on and on, into ever higher and finer vibrations. These ever higher levels of love go into spiritual realms far beyond my physical comprehension. This is the way of infinite love. It is pure white light, incorporating and penetrating all that is. Even if the lower levels of vibration do not comprehend the higher ones, they are still present. What hope this brings!

Picture of draconic Leo
At a physical level, this picture is very simple: a ring of gold surrounding pearly white paint that has not photographed well. The gold ring represents God, the source of infinite love. Inside this circle is iridescent white light. Everything that is in creation, all life, is encompassed by everything that God is, which is everything. The simplicity of the picture is parallel to the simplicity of the profound experience at an inner level of consciousness in the meditation. Words can hardly portray it. I think that by remaining with the simplicity of the picture and thinking the one word 'Love', a person is better able to feel what this meditation was about.

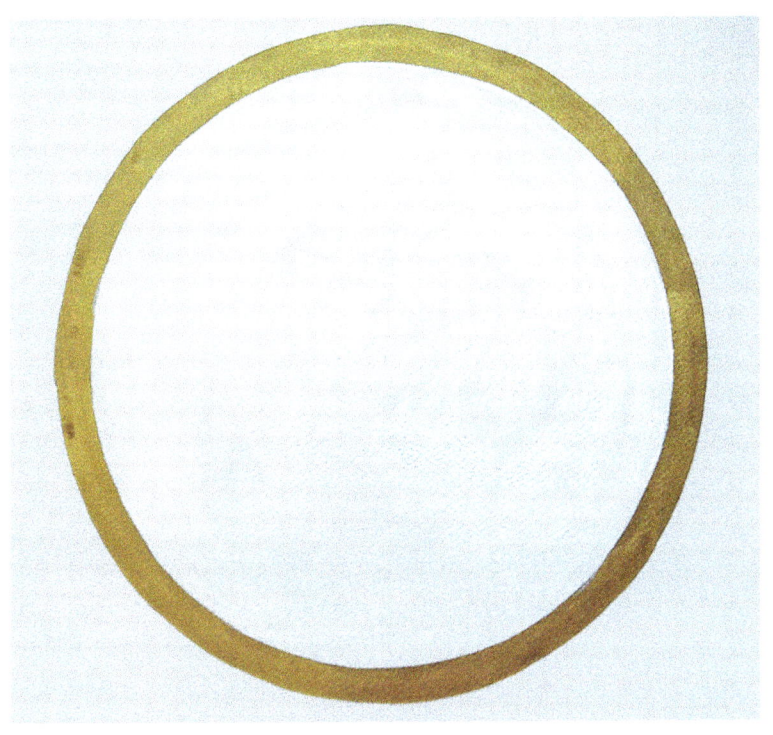

Figure 20. Draconic Leo

Summary of draconic Leo
I am in everything. I am everything.
I am the Life in every cell.
Spiritual Sun.
Pure White Light.

Comments
Tropical Leo is big-hearted and generous but likes respect and acknowledgement of individuality. Draconic Leo relates to acknowledgement of the true self: the spirit in a human body.

DRACONIC VIRGO

At the beginning of this meditation, I am surrounded by White Brothers. I am taken to a spring green rectangular crystal that is like a peridot. The crystal is golden spring green inside. This is an inner level of light that is different from the external colour of the crystal.

The crystal opens up to golden light coming from the heavens. As more golden light comes down, it feels as if the Source, Creator, God, is coming to Earth. I then start to float up into the source of that light. It feels like floating up to a heavenly creator. There was so much warmth and love in the source of light.

In this Source the hands of the source of life are holding the world. The hands are teaching and correcting the world, bringing it ever closer to the perfection of Source. There is a gentle feeling of steadily correcting the actions of humankind; gently showing humanity a more loving and wiser way to be.

Figure 21. Draconic Virgo

Picture of draconic Virgo
The outer golden circle represents God holding all of humanity in love. The six coloured circles surrounded by silver are facets of humanity and life on Earth. The inner golden circle surrounding amethyst represents the perfect wisdom of God. Each facet of life on Earth is learning that wisdom while being held in the love of God.

Summary of draconic Virgo
The source of golden light, holding the world, teaching it, correcting it.
Draconic Virgo is Golden Light pouring down to Earth.
Earth is held in God.
Earth is adapting, moving to the Perfection of God.

Comments
Tropical Virgo has an eye for detail and is analytical. This is part of seeking perfection but can also manifest as being critical. Draconic Virgo also relates to seeking perfection through gentle correction as the soul strives towards the ever-evolving perfection of Source.

DRACONIC LIBRA
There is a White Brother on the left-hand side of the tunnel entrance. There is another White Brother on the right-hand side just before I go from the tunnel into the cave. As I enter the cave, there is a crescent of White Brothers and the two from the tunnel come and complete the circle. Today, the White Brothers are more like people, with smiling faces, rather than Beings of light. I feel I know them and recognise their individuality. It is lovely to be so aware of them and feel their love. I feel that I am included in their circle to be shown something to bring to Earth.

I go up an aquamarine crystal tube that divides into Gemini and Libra. Libra is one limb, reaching out to Gemini, the other limb of the crystal, and then reaching all around.

A bulge of gold forms at the end of the Libra limb of the crystal. It is like a light bulb that lights the area. The light bulb feels contained but then bursts open to contact the area all around. This may represent my consciousness as it expands beyond the three-dimensional level of the physical world.

Gold and blue interpenetrate. It is like golden petals of a sunflower against blue sky. The sky is close to the centre of the sunflower. What is outside is close to what is in the centre and the centre understands what is going outside. There is an innate knowing of what is there without having to exchange words.

This level of understanding expands so that the centre can understand the Masters and feel part of them. 'I am in the Masters and they are in me.' At a higher level of consciousness, the interpenetration of different levels of life is experienced. This pattern is repeated going to higher and higher levels of consciousness, of life. It is like being in the centre that is God and being surrounded by God. 'I am in God and God is in me.' There is complete interpenetration of all levels, a sense of oneness, in this meditation.

When there is acceptance of the interpenetration of different levels of life, there can be complete understanding and harmony. Libra is linked with understanding 'other', which often means another person. It can also mean connections with other parts of life. This can include the body–mind–soul connection. Another thought that arose during contemplation concerns the spirit of soul, which is something other than soul but not spirit. Impulses from spirit to soul may be the soul's aspirations and guidance.

Figure 22. Draconic Libra

Picture of draconic Libra
This simple picture brings the sense of harmony and balance that is associated with Libra. However, each part of the above meditation is represented in it.

Within each 'petal' there are three levels: the silver line, the white between the silver and blue areas, and the blue areas. All of these parts contact the centre although I could not paint this as finely as I wished. When I painted the picture, the silver parts were one level of life, the white parts represented the Masters and the blue parts represented God. However, when I look at this picture longer, it seems to shift in interpretation. After a while, I think that the white parts, both within the petals and around the outside of them, are God. When I am in this state of consciousness, the silver parts become the Masters and the blue parts are God as well as physical life. This may seem confusing but it all seems perfectly all right while it is happening. Perhaps this phenomenon in itself shows how all life is interpenetrating and what one sees or experiences depends on the state of the observer.

This concept can help with understanding how the energy of Libra wants to harmonise things that appear to be different or even divergent and, through doing so, make sense of them.

Summary of draconic Libra
The centre understands that which is all around because it is the centre.
I am in God and God is in me.

Comments
Tropical Libra is associated with finding peace through harmonising different factions. At the draconic level, this

quality is extended to a much deeper level, that of knowing what each party experiences, which can affect the choice of actions taken.

DRACONIC SCORPIO

I go along the tunnel into the cave. At the far end is a large red light and the White Brothers are pushing me into this light. From the light, I can go up or down. Down goes into the 'hell' of earthly life as seen from the earthly, lower point of view: the earthly difficulties, materialism and fears. The possibility of going down into this 'hell' feels 'bad'. In contrast, going up goes into heaven. This feels better although it still does not feel absolutely right as I might miss learning something of value by experiencing earthly life.

I realise each choice would take me in a loop back to where I began. This suggests that it is the experience of the journey that is important and all journeys, all incarnations, together bring to the soul the wisdom it is seeking.

By looking up, I see that when things end their energy breaks up and regroups into the beginning of something new of a different form. When this happens on the same level of life it is called transformation. In this meditation, alchemy is when the breaking up of energy on one level is used for the beginning of something on another level.

Endings and beginnings, transformation and alchemy are all associated with Pluto, one of the rulers of Scorpio. Mars, the co-ruler of Scorpio, provides the energy to drive through the changes.

From a physical perspective, transformation and alchemy are mysteries. A deeper level of Scorpio signifies the desire to understand the mysteries of transformation and alchemy. An even deeper level seeks to know God, the Divine Power, Wisdom and Love. This is often beyond what can be understood by the earthly mind of humankind. The Almighty Presence is all Wisdom and all Love and has the Divine Power to bring about the mysteries and drive the changes.

From this it is easy to understand why there are three symbols of Scorpio: the scorpion at the physical level, the eagle at a higher level and the phoenix rising out of the ashes at an even higher level. Progression from one level to another may be linked to the written symbol of the sign as described in the explanation of Figure 23.

There may be even more dimensions to Scorpio that I do not understand. I also feel that there may be other dimensions to the other signs of the zodiac. In one way, this book is trying to explore these levels through the differences between tropical and draconic interpretations of the signs but I feel it is far more complex than this in a way that a three-dimensionally orientated human mind cannot comprehend. I am only beginning to be aware of the possibility that such a multi-dimensional interpretation of the signs exists.

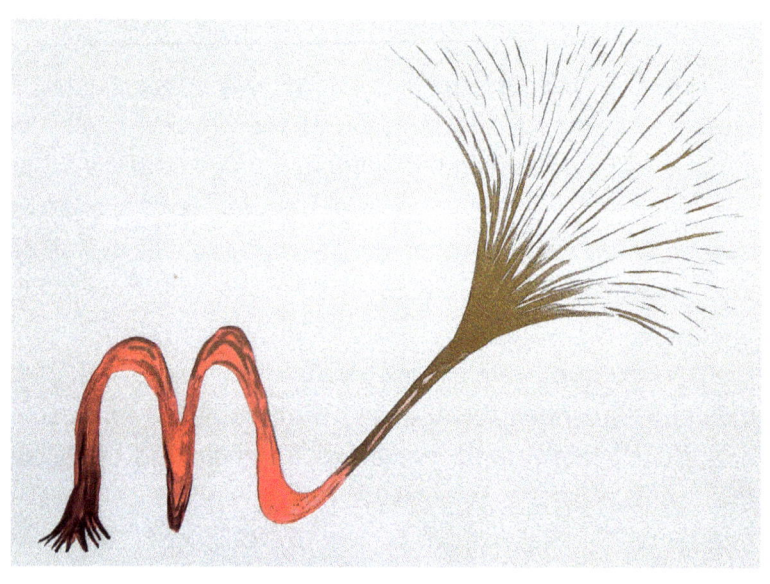

Figure 23. Draconic Scorpio

Picture of draconic Scorpio
In the bottom left-hand corner of the picture are the roots, dark and heavy, that hold mankind down to the material, physical level of life. This includes the difficulties, hardships and fears that appear to trap humanity here. However, the nature of mankind is to rise into the light so the person rises up out of the darkness; it becomes lighter. This is indicated by the change from dark maroon to lighter red and with the introduction of slivers of golden light. This gets lighter and brighter as the person reaches the top of the symbol on the left-hand side.

However, things can appear to drag the person down and a little more darkness creeps in. This state is shown pictorially by the slightly darker colours and absence of gold at the bottom of the middle of the 'M' of the symbol. It is a temporary state and again the person is able to rise up into the light and things are lighter and brighter than last time. There is more golden light.

Once again, something can happen and the person seems to be dragged down again but it is less dark than in the previous dip. This cycle of aspiration and falling back can happen many times as the soul evolves. It is like a spiral and although a soul may appear, sometimes, to be going backwards, I believe that the wisdom so gained contributes to the overall development of that soul.

Finally, with effort, a person is able to rise above all the darkness, which has been mastered. The person can ascend into golden light and is completely free of all the heaviness of the past experiences. Having left the constraints of material and physical life, the person is free to expand into worlds not known to the man or woman of Earth. The soul is free of the bondage of matter and becomes a master of alchemy but with the love and wisdom to know how to use it for good. The heavens are infinite and eternal.

Summary of draconic Scorpio
Transformation and alchemy are parts of the mysteries of life but the real mystery is what drives the changes.
Almighty Presence is a Great Might that is all-wisdom, all-love, and has the power to drive changes.
Draconic Scorpio is the drive to know the mysteries of life, to understand alchemy, to understand God.

Comments
Tropical Scorpio is associated with going beneath the surface of life's experiences. This can lead to transformation and regeneration. Draconic Scorpio also relates to transformation but at a far deeper level. It seeks the mysteries of life.

DRACONIC SAGITTARIUS
From the cave I go up through the tropical plane and into the next plane. I then go through a black hole which contains everything but I do not know what the 'everything' is. I can look in two directions, east and west, to the rising Sun and the setting Sun.

A horse appears and climbs up into the Sun. As horses are associated with Sagittarius, I think this meditation is on draconic Sagittarius. The horse puts its head down so that the plane of its forehead is vertical and touching what looks like the forehead of an enormous Buddha. This figure feels like a supreme Being.

At the point on the horse where the base of the horn of a unicorn would be there is a two-inch diameter area of white light that is connected to the forehead of the Buddha figure. Through this portal, information can flow in both directions: from the supreme Being to the horse and from the horse to the supreme Being. I feel that, perhaps at a higher level or dimension, this is the mind of God passing wisdom and love, guidance on how to act, to the higher mind of man and that this can ultimately be passed on to the lower mind and manifest as actions in daily life on Earth.

I can pass through the portal and go into the dimension and plane of consciousness of white light. Here I can see in all directions at once, and while the lower mind thinks in terms of travelling to different experiences this is not necessary as on this plane I can see everything all around. I can look down and see how things are connected. This is the plane of absolute and infinite truth. Here there is infinite wisdom and love. These are qualities vital to the integrity of Sagittarius.

Experience in this meditation may increase awareness of my 'third eye', the chakra that connects the physical body to the higher mind. It allows greater awareness of the finer planes of life that I experience as impressions of light. These are quite different from the mundane details of earthly life although I believe they are all integrally connected.

This meditation is about contact with the higher mind.

Figure 24. Draconic Sagittarius

Picture of draconic Sagittarius
This picture represents passing from the portal into the white light of the higher plane of consciousness. The light opens up in all directions and is infinite. It goes on and on, like a fountain of infinite wisdom. The fountain goes beyond the top of the picture and this represents wisdom being limitless. The blue and silver parts of the fountain represent the interpenetrating facets of this world.

Summary of draconic Sagittarius
The forehead touches the forehead of God.
Flow of Divine Wisdom.
The clarity of Truth, absolute and infinite Light.
All-wisdom, all-love.

Comments
The physical and mental freedom so loved by tropical Sagittarius expands into striving for infinite truth and wisdom at the draconic level.

DRACONIC CAPRICORN
I go up the mountain, through the tunnel and into the cave. I am welcomed by White Brothers. There is a deep red, spiky crystal at the back of the cave. It is made up of many thin, elongated diamond-shaped crystals that fit together. The deep red of the crystals brings a feeling of grandeur, which links with the way Capricorn can enjoy status at the physical level. This meditation is on draconic Capricorn.

I pass through the centre of one of the many crystals. Here there is absolute calm. Here there is no desire for respect. This is interesting as tropical Capricorn likes respect.

In the meditation, respect can be given and felt but without the desire for it.

From this point, I go up into the light and become aware of the hierarchy of the angels and of lower and higher states in the angelic kingdom. Somehow everything is inter-related and comfortable with the inter-relationships. I become aware that there are 'structures' in the heavens. These different 'structures' are different dimensions and states of consciousness. They all fit together like a multi-dimensional jigsaw puzzle. All worlds fit together. They can be differentiated but are not separate. There is a continuum. There is known order in this continuum. There is direction to all parts of life. The order and direction of everything comes from and is of God.

In the meditation, it feels like there is something higher than what humans call God, and something higher than that and higher than that, *ad infinitum*. This is a mind-expanding thought as the highest concept that I have is of God. I see many galaxies and the universe and feel this represents the physical parallel to the expanding scale of my awareness in meditation. In this multi-dimensional 'everythingness', there is absolute stillness that reaches into all parts of it. The stillness is light.

Each part of this giant, multi-dimensional jigsaw, each 'world', acts as a lens for light into other parts, other worlds. Each lens can be likened to a facet of a diamond that can reflect light from the inside of it back into the diamond or from the outside of it out in other directions that are outside the diamond. What happens within one part of life affects other parts in that dimension as well as other dimensions.

It feels as if the highest level of Capricorn knows all of the different structures, dimensions and parts of the multi-dimensional jigsaw. This might be at a higher, finer level than the one I had thought of as being the draconic level of Capricorn. God knows the order and structure of everything as well as every interaction between all of the different parts. Earthly life is one of these many parts.

When reflecting on this meditation later, it seemed that the many parts of the deep red crystal at the outset of the meditation resemble the many different worlds fitting together. All of life is interconnected.

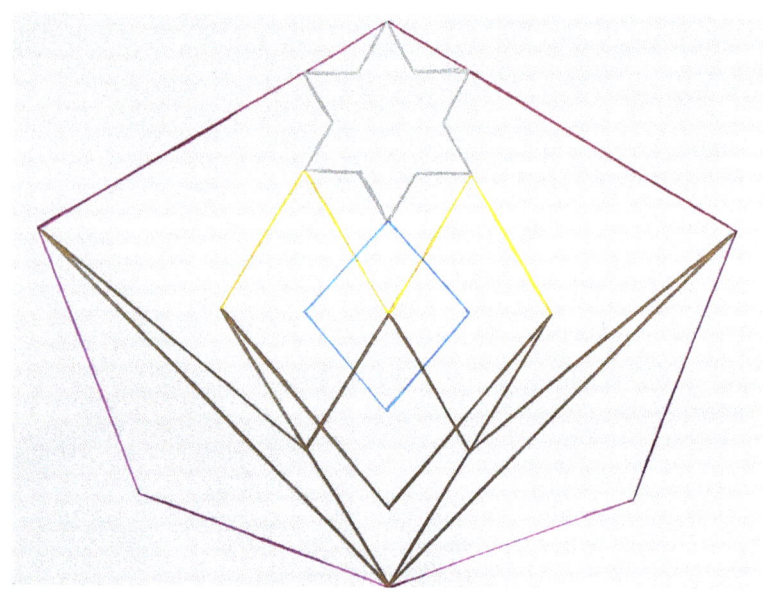

Figure 25. Draconic Capricorn

Picture of draconic Capricorn

When drawing this picture in pencil, the star was at the bottom. From the star, the rest of the picture represented the many levels of life that go above the physical plane of existence and how that tries to interact with higher planes. There were many more lines in the pencil drawing, showing many more interconnections between parts of life. However, when I started painting over the pencil lines, the orientation of the picture did not feel right and I had to turn it upside down so that the star was at the top. Perhaps this represents the pinnacle of what humanity can reach at this stage of its evolution.

The star is contained within the framework. The gold lines at the bottom look a bit like a stylised lotus, which opens and supports all other structures in the picture. This can be likened to God supporting all life. The outer, purple lines also feel like God, but this is now containing all life. In some way, the blue diamond in the centre feels like the Masters who are connecting the star to humanity. The yellow lines also connect the star to humankind but in a different way and I do not know what the difference means.

This is a very structured picture representing the many 'structures', the many dimensions, of life. They all have their individual roles to play and they are all interconnected. It is a simple and stylised pictorial representation of life that goes far beyond my physical comprehension.

Summary of draconic Capricorn

Each world acts as a lens for light into other worlds.
All dimensions of all worlds fit together like a multi-dimensional jigsaw.

God impulses know the order, direction and structure of everything, and how it all fits together, directing earthly life through the soul.

Comments
The structure and organisation of physical life associated with tropical Capricorn is extended in the draconic zodiac to include the structure and organisation of all levels of all dimensions of life.

DRACONIC AQUARIUS
The dual nature of the rulers of Aquarius is felt from the beginning of this meditation. One part starts at the top of the mountain, close to the Sun. The Sun is often thought of as the source of physical life. Uranus, one of the co-rulers of Aquarius, is sometimes called the 'truth- and light-bringer'. I feel that Uranus links with the spiritual counterpart of the Sun, the spiritual Sun. This is the source of spiritual light, love, wisdom and power. The second part starts by going along the tunnel into the cave. This duality continues with an awareness of light signifying Uranus and its connection to the Sun, but with an amethyst representing Saturn.

From the far side of the cave, a small dark amethyst, hidden away in a corner, opens into light that is so strong and bright that even in meditation I cannot look into it. A cube of amethyst moves into this light to give the light structure but then the cube opens up and light streams from it. The light and the cube work together. This can be interpreted in different ways: the cube sometimes represents physical life and here light is within matter and emerges from it. Another interpretation is that what has no form is one with what has form. (I acknowledge amethyst is a trigonal crystal and not a cube but that is how it appears in the meditation.)

The blazing light, which is far beyond human comprehension, represents the light and truth of God. It encompasses the universe known from Earth and many other universes, levels of life and spiritual concepts that mankind cannot even imagine. Uranus channels this light and truth.

The cube represents Saturn, which has the wisdom and the means to earth the light and truth. In order to bring the energy of the light and truth to a level that humans can assimilate, it has to be limited, stepped down and given a structure that can be related to the three dimensions of physical life. This is a form of discipline and is linked with Saturn.

In this way Uranus and Saturn work together to bring to Earth the wisdom, love and power of the spiritual Sun. Uranus is working with Saturn, Pluto and the Sun

Figure 26. Draconic Aquarius

Picture of draconic Aquarius
The purple cross in the centre is an amethyst that had the form of a cube but opened out. The white circle in the centre of the cross represents God and light is streaming out from this circle, through the arms of the cross out into all of life. The light goes into and through all that is.

Summary of draconic Aquarius
A cube moves into the Light giving it structure.
The cube opens as a cross and light comes out of the centre. The Truth of God.
Uranus channels the Light and Truth of God, helping humanity to access what is beyond human comprehension. Saturn helps people to learn about this by giving it structure.

Comments
Tropical Aquarius strives to live truth through objectivity, originality and independence. Truth is taken to a far deeper level in the draconic zodiac. This is the truth and light of God that goes beyond human comprehension.

DRACONIC PISCES
The cave is filled with light and I am greeted by White Brothers. I squeeze through an opening near the top of the roof of the cave and could go into white light and blue sky but I hang on to the roof of the cave. It feels as if am fearful of letting go. I wonder what would happen to me if I were to let go. It feels as if letting go would be a sacrifice and there is some fear of going into unknown realms. This reminds me of Pisces and I realise this meditation is on draconic Pisces.

I expand and become one with the whole of Earth, including the mountain and cave. There are no boundaries between me and these things. The breaking down of boundaries is also characteristic of Pisces. I am now able to let go and I float and continue to expand, to the Brothers on the planets, to all of the universe and many other levels as well as down to Earth. It feels as if I am becoming one with the physical Earth, the Beings of the planets and many other dimensions. I am one with all life. As I breathe, life breathes. As life breathes, I breathe. There is no separation. All is of God. Neptune is a link between humanity and God. It is the planet that helps mankind know unity with God.

Picture of draconic Pisces
The diffuse and nebulous nature of the colours that flow gently into one another represents the life and light that flow through and penetrate all that is. Nothing is really separate. At some level, every single thing, whether seen or unseen, touches and merges with all other things. The silver swirling lines show how everything is connected with everything else, emphasising the nature of non-separation. God is in everything. The difference between the diffuse colours and the defined lines represents the difference between the various levels of life. Just as the lines go over the colours, so the different levels of life interpenetrate each other.

Figure 27. Draconic Pisces

Summary of draconic Pisces
Expanding into all of the universe, many universes, many levels.
At one with everything.
At one with all life.
Breathing with all life.
Expanding beyond all life.
Neptune – a cup filled with God by God.

Comments
Kindness and compassion associated with tropical Pisces come from being sensitive and intuitive. Tropical Pisces can feel what other people feel. Draconic Pisces extends the transcendental qualities of tropical Pisces to encompass all levels of life, known and unknown.

Chapter 5

Review

This section is called a review. It is not a summary, which would be a précised repetition of what has been presented. It is not a conclusion because that word implies that something has ended and deductions may be drawn. The study of draconic astrology has not ended and any deductions drawn within this text are only from my current knowledge and awareness. This section is a review that looks at what has been accomplished and how draconic astrology could further unfold.

The difference between the tropical and draconic horoscopes can vary enormously. The two horoscopes can be very similar if the tropical north node of the Moon is close to 0° Aries, either at the end of Pisces or in the early degrees of Aries. When the draconic and tropical charts are very similar, I believe that the soul's impulses are strongly aligned to the outer life. This enables the person to bring the soul's purpose into physical manifestation.

In contrast, if the tropical north node of the Moon is close to 0° Libra, the tropical and draconic horoscopes are totally different. Planets and angles fall in the opposite signs of the zodiac in the two horoscopes. When there are roughly 180° between the tropical and draconic charts, the soul's impulses are guiding the outer life in a totally different way from what is happening in the outer life. The soul's impulses and the outer life are operating from two different and apparently disparate energies. Although it sounds as if this could create inner tension, it also provides an opportunity for the person to learn how to integrate and blend these energies. This brings a wide spectrum of experience.

These are the two extremes of alignment between the tropical and draconic horoscopes. There are many variations in between and each is interpreted as a unique combination experienced by that person.

What has emerged from looking at the tropical as well as the draconic horoscopes of individuals is that, in some cases, the soul has elected to do something at a soul level but this has worked out in an apparently different way at a physical level. Here are some examples:

- A person who is an explorer or adventurer at the outer level as shown by the tropical horoscope may be wanting to undergo profound transformation at a soul level, which could be seen in the draconic chart. Exploration is the avenue the soul chose to gain this inner experience.
- A person may have an interest in a political career in physical life, while at an inner level he or she is more concerned with the brotherhood of humanity. The tropical chart could indicate political aspirations but the draconic chart could indicate greater humanitarian or utopian interests.
- A scientist with an apparent interest in the physical sciences may be guided by a soul that cares deeply for the plight of humankind. The person could manifest their soul's humanitarian impulses, shown by the

draconic horoscope, through careful and studious scientific research that is seen in the tropical horoscope.
- A composer or musician may be very particular in their work, as seen in the tropical horoscope. However, the draconic horoscope may suggest that the soul could be receiving impulses from higher realms of life. This person is able to bring beautiful, inspired music down to earth. The same can apply to artists.

In every case, it is always worth checking if a planet has a specific affiliation to the sign it occupies such as dignity or exaltation, detriment or fall, in one or other of the horoscopes. A planet might be in dignity in the tropical horoscope but not the draconic one, and vice versa. This affects the interpretations. Furthermore, as shown in the descriptions of the meditations, their interpretation can differ notably between the tropical and draconic zodiacs.

During the course of the meditations, I have often thought that I am just touching the surface of something that is extensive; the tip of the iceberg. I feel that draconic astrology will go far deeper in due course. What I have written in this book has depended on my own stage of development and sensitivity at the time of doing this work.

When using interpretations from the meditations to look at the draconic charts of individuals, there have been many times when I have thought that the draconic chart has given possible insights into previous lives. Sometimes it has felt as if these individuals have come back to finish a piece of work started in another lifetime. There are many cases in which it feels as if the soul's impulses are guiding the soul towards greater interest in the welfare of all life rather than personal gain.

I feel that the biggest potential for draconic astrology is to help humankind understand the inner level of life and what the soul wants to learn through experiences in physical life. Draconic astrology is a tool to access deeper and deeper levels of the human being. Ultimately, astrology may go beyond consideration of the soul's impulses to focus primarily on a person's spirit and its role in the whole of life. So much depends on the stage of evolution of the human race as well as that of both the astrologer and the client at the time of a consultation.

There is no doubt in my mind that the inner work done by astrologers will be the way forward for astrology as it goes beyond what it can do today. As astrologers become more sensitive to inspiration from higher worlds, the interpretations of charts will evolve. Not only will this go hand in hand with the evolution of humanity as a species but also with increased awareness that humanity is only one of the many lifeforms in creation.

Some further thoughts
Descriptions of the mediations on the planets and signs of the zodiac have been illustrated with paintings. Now, in a deep and peaceful state of awareness but not in meditation, a further image has come to mind.

The following picture has three rings of coloured circles. In the outermost ring, the twelve circles are separate. This feels like the separation experienced at a physical level. Many people compartmentalise life into work, family, friends, money and so on. In addition, many people see themselves as separate from other people. Many also think they are separate from higher levels of life, even if they acknowledge that such things exist.

In the next ring of twelve circles, each is encircled by silver and joined on either side by silver links. This ring represents the twelve signs of the tropical zodiac. This shows how the different parts of the life of a person are linked and can be looked at in the tropical horoscope. At this level, some people are beginning to appreciate interconnectedness not only to other people but also to other levels of life.

Each of the coloured circles in the innermost ring of circles is encircled by gold. These circles touch each other. This ring represents the draconic level of astrology. At this level, the soul is aware of the connections within itself, to others and to other levels of life.

The coloured circles are the same colours in each of the rings but they get paler going from the outermost ring to the innermost one. This depicts how life on the inner planes is finer and more subtle, at least as seen from the physical perspective.

At the centre of these circles is a solid ring in gold representing spirit. Inside that ring is a pure white circle that represents God. Although at the physical level of life humans can appear to be separate from God, God is at the centre of all that is. God is in and around everything just as there is white paper around all the coloured parts of this picture. This picture attempts to show the different levels of life but I acknowledge that it is a very simple picture and cannot possibly depict life in total when it is an image created with physical materials.

Figure 28. Life

www.ingramcontent.com/pod-product-compliance
Lightning Source LLC
Chambersburg PA
CBHW041925090426
42743CB00020B/3446